Life's Philosophy

Life's Philosophy

REASON & FEELING IN A DEEPER WORLD

Arne Naess

with Per Ingvar Haukeland

Translated by Roland Huntford

with a foreword by Bill McKibben

& an introduction by Harold Glasser

The University of Georgia Press *Athens & London*

Originally published in Norwegian in 1998 by Universitetsforlaget with the title
Livsfilosofi: Et personlig bidrag om følelser og fornuft.

Translation published by the University of Georgia Press, Athens, Georgia 30602

© 2002 by Arne Naess

Foreword © 2002 by Bill McKibben

Introduction © 2002 by Harold Glasser

Designed by Kathi Dailey Morgan

Set in 10.3 on 14 Minion by Bookcomp

Printed and bound by Maple-Vail

The paper in this book meets the guidelines for permanence and durability
of the Committee on Production Guidelines for Book Longevity of the
Council on Library Resources.

Printed in the United States of America

06 05 04 03 02 C 5 4 3 2 1

Library of Congress Cataloging-in-Publication Data

Naess, Arne.

[Livsfilosofi. English]

Life's philosophy : reason and feeling in a deeper world / Arne Naess
with Per Ingvar Haukeland ; translated by Roland Huntford ; with a foreword
by Bill McKibben ; and an introduction by Harold Glasser.

p.   cm.

ISBN: 0-8203-2418-3 (alk. paper)

1. Conduct of life. I. Haukeland, Per Ingvar, 1966–. II. Title.

BJ1588.N6 N4713 2003

198'.1—dc21   2001008020

British Library Cataloging-in-Publication Data available

To my wife, Kit-Fai, who made it all possible

I would like to thank my friend Per Ingvar Haukeland, who, in his capacity as my assistant for this book project, helped me to organize a vast amount of material. He worked through pages of notes I had accumulated through a decade on subjects relevant to this book. Our many conversations, especially those that took place in the stillness of Tvergastein, were invaluable.

My editor at the Scandinavian University Press, Knut Olav Aamaas, has played a vital role. In a long series of discussions, he displayed an unbounded interest, which has influenced the contents of this book, and finally the structure as well.

CONTENTS

A book by the title *Life's Philosophy* would normally be fair game for ridicule. It sounds just a tad egoistic—what's the Norse for "chutzpah"? But in this case the author is first of all an actual card-carrying philosopher, indeed one of great renown, and he has lived an actual life, one that by every indication has verged on the splendid. And so in this case the title turns out to be the utter opposite of pretentious, as is the book—in fact, they lack pretense almost entirely, as if written in some altogether forgotten language where arrogance is not a linguistic possibility.

Americans who know of Arne Naess (and, given that he is a Norwegian philosopher, a surprising number do) know of him because of his connection with the environmental debate—most significantly, his work with Californian George Sessions to formulate the principles of Deep Ecology. As this book makes clear, those completely sane and modest (albeit revolutionary) principles come from a sane and modest mind, albeit one out of step with the times. Here is a defense of slow learning, of joyfulness, of simplicity, of listening to faint feelings, that contradicts nearly every notion of a "successful" modern life.

And yet, just as one cannot read Wendell Berry without wishing to become a small farmer, one cannot read this book without wanting to turn into some emotional semblance of its author—to marry the strong Scandinavian sense of reason with the strong Scandinavian love of nature (all those Norwegians in their rustic cabins!), and to grace it with an exquisite mindfulness. Here is the examined life, but not the excoriated one: there is a tenderness in Naess, especially in his regard for the young and their education, that is too rare among our elders. His seems to be a life without bitter aftertaste.

Indeed, he offers a volume that sometimes seems to me a *Strunk and White* for daily life: "To Learn Well Is to Learn Slowly"; "Music Conveys Emotion Better than Words"; "Do Little Things in a Big Way." His ending, with its mathematical endorsement of fervor, will linger in your mind.

Very few people, I fear, change their lives as a result of reading contemporary academic philosophy. They are more likely to respond to example, to story. So here is a kind of universal great-grandfather, eager to share some gentle wisdom about that most mystifying of topics: How to Live. It is a grand and generous gift.

Bill McKibben

As I approach my ninetieth year, I may justifiably claim to have seen life. And looking back, I am surprised at how often I have been driven by strong feelings. For example, they led to my collecting big numbers before I started school. There was something about big numbers that fascinated me, and in my innocence I thought that they were finite in number! All in all, I felt a profound attraction to the abstract and to what lay far off. On that account I subsequently took a degree in astronomy.

It was only as a professor that I became aware of the difficulties of suppressing the significance of the development of feelings in human affairs while at the same time worshiping reason. Both are constantly needed. As a result, in this book I am not trying to undermine reason by emphasizing feeling. Rather, I have an urge to try new ways of understanding how they belong to each other, and also to resort to old ways, with the help of my most important model as a philosopher of feelings, Spinoza.

Life may be considered as a landscape through which we travel in different ways. That journey on which I would like to take the reader starts out from today's crude and indefensible underestimation of the development of feelings in life and society; our destination is an awareness of the decisive role that feelings play, indeed ought to play, in human thought and action.

But is it not more important to live than to read about someone else's reflections on living? That goes without saying. The difficulty is that very many people reflect too little on their own life, and many begin to do so all too late. If this book can persuade some more, perhaps only a few, to reexamine their own existence and the direction of their lives, I will have achieved my aim. There is a difference between simply *functioning* as a human being and realizing that it is *now that one is living.*

It is strange how one opens oneself more to life when death is no longer something alien and threatening. That one's life may end today can lead to a more intense feeling of how significant that day is. There is something fundamentally wrong when only older people reflect on that which is significant in life, while younger ones, who have their lives before them, simply have no time to do so. They often have so much to do, so many goals, big and small, that they do not have time or opportunity to reflect on what is almost incredible: that today they actually are in the land of the living. And that the others surrounding them are their fellow creatures and human beings like themselves.

Life's Philosophy is not a professional treatise; it is a short book on a few themes that are important for me personally, themes in which emotions are the point of departure and the focus of the whole. In many ways I do not consider myself particularly qualified to write a book like this—at any rate no more competent than anyone who has lived and thought a little.

This is a book in which the questions considerably outnumber the answers. My aim is to give at least one person some good ideas, some thoughts to consider further, some new questions to ask himself and his closest friends. Best of all, perhaps he might be persuaded to consider his own existence in new ways.

Arne Naess
Oslo, October 1998

> The intellect is powerless to express thought without the aid of the
> heart and liver and of every member. . . .
>
>   . . . A man thinks as well through his legs and arms as his brain.
> We exaggerate the importance and exclusiveness of the headquarters.
> Do you suppose they were a race of consumptives and dyspeptics
> who invented Grecian mythology and poetry? The poet's words are,
> "You would almost say the body thought!" I quite say it.
>
>   HENRY DAVID THOREAU, *Journals*

For many who feel an affinity with life, the Earth, once ever
bountiful, is now increasingly checkered with wounds and despair.
In the midst of unprecedented economic growth, a general pauper-
ization and homogenization of both culture and nature abound.
We are smack in the middle of our planet's sixth great extinction
crisis, and this time we are the perpetrators. There is no simple,
single cause. Since at least the age of the Sumerians, humans have
brought about large-scale abuse of the Earth and each other. The
rate of change, the magnitude, and the complexity of our present situation, however, are unprecedented. Population growth, consumption, commodification, technology, globalization, and a tangled web
of other ostensibly autonomous, out-of-control factors all seemingly
conspire to quell the evolutionary process. Our healing efforts—
cooked up using a narrow, trite notion of rationality—frequently

amount to quenching a blaze by fueling the fire. Taking this picture in, it is easy to feel numbed into inaction.

Arne Naess is a ray of sunshine, a beacon of hope, in what for many has become a melancholic world. This is not because he views our society and the Earth's condition in a fundamentally different way. He doesn't. He is fond of saying that he is pessimistic about the twenty-first century but optimistic about the twenty-second. What makes Naess so unusual is that he also reminds us, unrelentingly, in his spritelike way, that we live in a world of unsurpassed wonder, beauty, and possibility. It is a world worth fighting—nonviolently— to save. Anything can happen. The future need not mirror the past. There is always reason for hope.

In *Life's Philosophy* Naess urges us to reflect on our values and to more securely anchor our actions to them. A fundamental tenet of his life philosophy is a firm belief that "we need to return to a perception that considers something rational and reasonable *only if* it appears to be so in relation to the broadest and deepest norms— those that are considered most essential for the individual and society" (p. 3). With a grin and an aura of great seriousness, he cajoles us to seek the center of conflict rather than mill around the periphery. At the same time, he implores us to strictly adhere to Gandhi's principles of nonviolence. Naess would have us cheerfully invite our adversaries over to tea and coffee; we should decry their unsustainable actions, not them. Everyone is a potential ally.

The ecocultural crisis is not merely a topic for academic bantering and internecine battles over the existence or nonexistence of the "intrinsic value" of nonhumans. We *feel* nature's wonder, joy, beauty, and possibility, so it exists. It is under fire, so we *must*, with all our might, fight for it. We fight for it because it exists *and* because we depend on it for our survival; because in its profound otherness lies a key to our own spiritual, emotional, and cultural development— our maturation process both as individuals and as a species; and because its loss is our loss. Hume's fact/value dichotomy is essentially sophistry. His separation of "facts" from "nonfacts," value-free descriptions from norms, rests on a false assumption—the existence of an ontological divide. Once this illusion is shattered, the divide vanishes and the distinction blurs forever.

Our ever clever and creative minds search for easy ways out of the ecocultural crisis. Our hearts remind us that no silver bullets exist. Try as we might, we cannot simply reason away poverty, inequity, climate change, loss of cultural diversity, soil depletion, impending fresh water shortages, acid rain, and the ozone hole. The force of Descartes's arguments notwithstanding, separate lives of pure cognition and feeling simply don't exist; they are integrated into one mind-body. We experience the world somatically and intellectually in concert as variously ordered, multilayered gestalts. As Thoreau asserts, the mind-body "separation" is yet another absurd dichotomization. Addressing the momentous problems before us, as with any creative pursuit, will demand the commitment of our entire beings.

The divorce of mind and body was plotted by Descartes to construct a parallel separation between science and theology. Tension was brewing between the newly successful mechanistic philosophy and the traditional religious establishment over their differing interpretations of the world. Descartes's vision was to relieve the ferment by dividing reality into two distinct realms. Nonthinking extended substance (body) would be the province of scientific investigation, while unextended thinking substance (mind or soul) would be the domain of theology. With this compartmentalization, potential conflicts between science and religion could be eliminated before they arose.

The division was successful beyond Descartes's wildest dreams, so much so that today science has in many ways trumped religion as the ultimate arbiter of reality. C. P. Snow's "two cultures" is one of the byproducts of Cartesian dualism. Snow, despite his cogent characterization of the dangerous rift between the sciences and the humanities, is content to maintain the separation as long as we cultivate an awareness and appreciation that connect the two realms. However admirable and desirable, Snow's proposal is simply not up to the task at hand. Even an "information superhighway" linking the realms merely bridges the divide, at best. The barriers that created the rift in the first place are not dismantled. Unlike the fall of the Berlin Wall or the dissolution of the Soviet Union, such a plan offers little hope for freeing people to think in fundamentally different ways. It is the very existence and persistence of such artificial dichotomies—mind/body, man/nature, fact/value, and, most important, reason/feeling—that is at issue, not Snow's important proposal to promote communication between scientists and humanists.

Descartes's error is analogous to the failure of the great free-market economist and cornucopian, Julian Simon, to recognize that, while more people certainly bring more minds to solve more problems, they also bring more mouths and stomachs to feed and fill, more needs and cravings to be fulfilled, and, ultimately, more waste to dispose of. The tradeoff of our relatively simple, scientific picture ·of the world—one that has given us tremendous power to manipulate the world—is that we are left with a fragmented, incomplete understanding of ourselves and nature. Our value-free, idealized notion of reason undermines our roots and promise. It severs us from our simian past, divides us from our feelings, diffuses our concern for community and the future, and, by encouraging the domination of nature, inevitably leaves both people and nature impoverished.

We can very likely survive in a world of plastic trees, but how will it affect us psychologically, spiritually, and physically?[1] How might such an increasingly technology-driven, homogenized world affect our prospects for moral, material, and social progress? Almost thirty years ago, E. F. Schumacher, former chief economist and head of planning at the British Coal Board and author of *Small Is Beautiful,* counseled, "Our reason has become beclouded by an extraordinary, blind and unreasonable faith in a set of fantastic and life-destroying ideas inherited from the nineteenth century. It is the foremost task of our reason to recover a truer faith than that."[2]

> Emotion is the source of all becoming-consciousness. There can be no transforming of darkness into light and of apathy into movement without emotion.
>
> C. J. JUNG, *Psychological Aspects of the Modern Archetype*

Perhaps no other philosopher of the twentieth century has gone further than Arne Naess has toward breaking the spell of "value-free" rationality, not by derogating the significance of reason, but rather by greatly expanding its ambit. Naess is not content with viewing rationality in purely instrumental terms—as simply an efficacious means to satisfy previously defined ends—as has become common-place today. A self-proclaimed worshiper of reason, Naess is also not interested in forsaking empirical analysis or the preciseness of science. As a small child he developed a tremendous resistance to emotion and cultivated a detached, scientific mode of expression as a reaction to his mother's sentimentality and emotional hysteria.[3] In his early twenties he was welcomed by the logical empiricists of the Vienna Circle, despite his opposition to their antimetaphysical stance and his leanings toward American pragmatism. Much of his early work was devoted to empirical explorations of terms such as *truth* and *democracy* and the search for a "science of science"—the multifaceted study of the scientific enterprise from outside, which strives to ground the construction and application of theory in log-ical and empirical research.[4]

The more mature Naess, a much more sophisticated student of human behavior and cultural anthropology, became further at-tuned to the shortcomings and potential pitfalls of a unified theory of science and philosophy. His dedication to the empirical approach and his concerns regarding philosophical dogmatism led him to a radical form of pluralism and possibilism informed by Pyrrhonic skepticism.[5] Naess's transition from scientism to philosophy and from the theory of scientific models to the theory of philosophical systems was motivated, in part, by two key concepts. *Possibilism* is the idea that anything can happen. We should take care in assuming that an increase in the uniformity of opinion regarding a theory or policy is a reliable indicator of increase in truth content—it may very well be an indicator of cultural homogenization, the urge to conform, or a host of other possibilities. *Pluralism* is the notion that an indefinite plurality of equally valid but mutually inconsistent or incompatible theories, approaches, or interpretations exists to address any problem or issue. More colloquially, pluralism refers to the idea that there are a rich variety of potential lifestyles and specific actions in concrete situations that are consistent with our broadest and deepest norms—our ultimate beliefs.

Using Naessian terminology, our entire beings experience the world as "concrete contents." Whether scientists or schoolteachers, poets, philosophers, or photographers, we can never truly communicate our spontaneous experiences in exactly the same way as we experience them ourselves. We do, however, learn to interpret the world and communicate about it through constructed entities, "abstract structures"—language, symbols, systems, models, logic, descriptions, pictures, analogies—windows on our experience. Feelings and emotions are the glue that inextricably marries "facts" to "values." They bind the world that is, with all its splendor and terror, to the world of our hopes, dreams, and imagination. Feelings and emotions are the source of our ideas, inspiration, and creativity: they are what enable us to reason deeply and they are what impel us to act. As Naess explains, "Reason loses its function where there is no motivation, and motivation is absent where there are no feelings either for or against" (p. 4).

In this, the latest book of Naess's some seventy years as a philosopher, he offers us a meditation on the "art of living." According to Naess, "it is a short book on a few themes that are important for me personally, themes in which emotions are the point of departure and the focus of the whole" (p. xii). Like Penelope in reverse, Naess creates a complex tapestry that weaves together key ideas from his principal works on Spinoza, Gandhi, skepticism, philosophy of science, semantics, communication theory, cultural anthropology, and environmental philosophy to address a single theme.[6] Naess is interested in what it means, both conceptually and practically, to "feel at home in life." In his inimitable, sometimes confounding yet keenly insightful fashion, he takes up the question of how to face life's many hurdles with delight, creativity, and aplomb. His inquiry revolves around two "vital challenges." First, what might it mean for us to listen to both reason and emotion simultaneously? Second, how can we learn to turn negative feelings into positive ones in a manner that enhances the quality of life for all beings and yields genuine happiness?

Naess's central assertion is that contemporary Western society, in its modernistic quest for detached objectivity, has largely displaced feeling and emotion and thus betrayed the true potential for a richer form of reason. We have overestimated the significance of high-status knowledge, particularly scientific and technical knowledge, for resolving vital questions that fall in the realm of politics, ethics, and social decision making. We have also systematically undermined the cognitive value of feelings and emotions—once viewed as essential to the cultivation of maturity and wisdom, and now recognized, in some circles, as fundamental to the creative process. Our conception of reason has become limited to fulfilling, at best, one or two narrow goals rather than following an appropriate deliberative process that necessitates satisfying a range of considerations, including the questioning of our goals and the values and assumptions they are based on. The betrayal of reason lies not with an inherent limitation of the concept itself, but rather in our mode of conceiving it as disembodied, decontextualized, and essentially decoupled from our feelings and emotions.

As children we learn (or rather, are directed), very early, to separate scientific knowledge and empirical facts from myth and subjective experience. As adults we tend to cultivate reason as analytic and logical problem-solving skills, but much of what we most care about, much of what makes life so worth living and such a miracle, is dependent on "subjective" experience—education, art, love, and relationship to community, family, and friends (human and nonhuman alike). Furthermore, we tend to view technology as a panacea that will be able to outpace biophysical reality, human greed, and all of the most unsavory aspects of human behavior. This hypothesis, however, remains largely untested. Despite our ostensible emphasis on empirical analysis, there is a general failure to measure effectively. For instance, we have yet to systematically assess the long-term effects of World Bank "development" projects on quality of life and environmental health, the realistic potential of prisons to rehabilitate criminals, or the relationship between continued technological growth and human emancipation. The highest form of the betrayal of reason is our continued profligate destruction of the planet for uncertain human benefit, while the data on ecocultural ruination continue to mount.

Life's Philosophy is essentially a clarion call, an exhortation, to consider the significance of remarkably expanding our concept of reason so that we may enhance our prospects for "achieving" the good life, the good society, and a healthy, ecoculturally diverse planet. Naess's proposal to integrate reason and emotion is meant to serve as a countercurrent to the nineteenth-century view of emotions. Darwin summed up that perspective in *The Expression of the Emotions in Man and Animals:* "He who gives way to violent gestures will increase his rage; he who does not control the signs of fear will experience fear in a greater degree; and he who remains passive when overwhelmed with grief loses his best chance of recovering elasticity of mind."[7] In Darwin's view, feelings and emotions are largely to be controlled and suppressed. He fails to recognize, however, that they can also be the finest, most sublime sources of inspiration, insight, and wisdom. In Naess's more visceral, harmonious view, informed by his study of human behavior, emotions and feelings enhance reason, rather than act in opposition to it. Supporting his perspective is a broad array of leading scientists and thinkers. Barbara McClintock, Konrad Lorenz, Albert Einstein, Carl Friedrich Gauss, Norbert Wiener, E. O. Wilson, and Michael Polanyi have all spoken openly of the irreplaceable role that feelings and emotions have played in their own creative development.[8] Another cadre of scientists and thinkers, including Paul Shepard, Aldo Leopold, Rachel Carson, Justice William O. Douglas, Theo Colborn, Michael Soulé, Donella Meadows, and Gary Paul Nabhan and Stephen Trimble, have blended a high level of emotional maturity with sophisticated analytical and logical reasoning to draw attention to conflicts between our actions and our fundamental aims, and thus have become some of the most effective advocates for sound, future-focused policy and action.[9]

In addressing the knottier question of how to turn negative feelings into positive ones, Naess draws his inspiration from Spinoza, who argues similarly that an absence of emotion induces a stagnation of development. Both also believe that humans are essentially good by nature. Furthermore, Naess's belief in possibilism prevents him from entertaining the existence of a priori limits to the perfectibility of humans. Humans can be a positive, creative force on Earth. And this, ultimately, makes him strongly committed to the Enlightenment ideal of social progress.[10] That is, as long as his proposal for redefining the standards for what constitutes rationality and rational decision making is followed: "something is not rational unless it corresponds with the fundamental values and aims of our lives" (p. 88). For Naess, this means having a feeling for, or identifying with, all life.

In Spinoza's view, we have *passive* or negative emotions, such as pessimism, apathy, and despair, and *active* or positive emotions, such as joy, liberty, and freedom. Active emotions engage our whole being and help us to develop our essential nature, while passive emotions do not. Spinoza's concept of *ratio,* roughly translated as "the voice of reason," integrates reason and emotion. It is akin to an inner compass that guides us in a manner that nurtures our active emotions. In Naess's view, negative emotions have no intrinsic value, but they do have significant instrumental value. They have an important role to play in our development, if they are deeply felt and properly directed. By calling our attention to a problem, they can help us to become active in relation to the problem and thus stimulate positive change. Tremendous power and freedom is released by tapping into the potential of positive emotions and feelings—they can help us to cultivate a deeper, richer understanding of ourselves and our relationship to the world.

Naess's radical pluralism, identification with all life, and commitment to the potential for human maturation make him see the present ecocultural crisis as a travesty. As Naess points out, "Decisions cannot wait until all the facts are gathered: they are never all available."[11] We can never have the complete information that the scientific model of rationality demands. The relevant questions should be "How can we act in a consistent and life-affirming manner in the face of uncertainty, risk, potential irreversibility, and lack of complete information? And how do we turn our life-destroying tendencies into life-affirming ones?" In the words of Thomas Berry, the great work before us is to learn how "to create a mutually enhancing mode of human dwelling on planet Earth."[12] In Naess's eyes, reintegrating reason and emotion is a first step.

Naess does not offer us a prepackaged solution—he is not presumptuous or naïve enough to try that; besides, it would be antithetical to his character. What he does do, however, is offer us a guidebook with a suite of new ways to look at things and a series of koans to help us to "find our own way"—*sva marga,* to use one of his favorite Sanskrit terms. If Naess can be said to offer one main suggestion, it is that "we ought to talk about how we feel about things, ourselves, and the world, more often and without qualms" (p. 54). In an interview with Bob Jickling, Naess outlines one possible strategy for initiating such discussions. He explains that introducing questions such as "How do you feel?" and "What do you feel?" inevitably leads to "What should you feel?" "What do you think you are right to feel?" and "What do you want yourself to feel?"[13] In this way, a hearty interest in fundamental questions and active engagement with the world naturally lead to sophisticated ethical analysis and help to cultivate emotional maturity. To facilitate fruitful communication involving emotional topics and reduce misunderstanding, Naess offers a set of six ethical rules for unbiased verbal communication, which are drawn from more than half a century of research on empirical semantics and communication practice.

Ultimately, Naess is calling for a reanimation of the world through a reembodiment of reason. He is calling for a new-old form of reason that embraces feelings and emotions, enabling mind and body, fact and value, nature and culture to be seamlessly integrated, thus transcending the false dichotomies discussed earlier. Wisdom comes into being only by nurturing emotional intelligence. Moving beyond our current state of arrested emotional intelligence and immaturity requires responding to the causes of alienation. To address the central causes of alienation, we must expand our perspective and cultivate a broader, richer form of reason that incorporates love, compassion, and identification with all life. In this way, reason and emotion form a mutually reinforcing symbiosis. And with the addition of joy and playfulness, the whole process springs to life.

> We reason deeply, when we forcibly feel.
>
> MARY WOLLSTONECRAFT, *Letters Written during a Short Residence in Sweden, Norway, and Denmark*

In Norway, Arne Naess is regarded as a national treasure, not simply one of the boldest and most provocative thinkers of the twentieth century. His radical pluralism and endorsement of diversity are mirrored by his own complex character. He has a proclivity for being both aloof and charming, somber and joyful, accountable and carefree. He strives for preciseness, yet he appreciates vagueness and eschews dogma, refusing to be pinned down to a particular viewpoint or placed in a particular philosophical camp. This stance is further supported by his sometimes maddening tendency to revise, revise, and re-revise. Naess stands out because his frequently outlandish and controversial views are deeply felt, carefully reasoned, and playfully conveyed. Naess is a troublemaker, but the kind of troublemaker everyone wants to have around—he challenges orthodoxies with an elfin irreverence. His engagement and picaresque, passionate joie de vivre embody Spinoza's distinction between mere *activity* and true *activeness*, and make him an inspiration for all.

The original Norwegian version of the book before you has sold 110,000 copies. In a country of fewer than 4.5 million people, that is roughly equivalent to selling 6.8 million books in the United States. Naess has had a profound influence on Norwegian philosophy and social research. From 1939 to 1954 he was the only professor of philosophy in Norway. He was chiefly responsible for organizing the courses for the *examen philosophicum*, required of all undergraduates. His unique paradigm of inquiry, emphasizing open-mindedness, a vital concern for contemporary problems, and a thorough grounding in philosophy and the history of ideas, is credited with shaping the intellectual fabric of postwar Norway. Although he has received a host of international awards for his contributions, including the Nordic Prize from the Swedish Academy (1996), the Mahatma Gandhi Prize for Non-violent Peace (1994), and the Sonning Prize for contributions to European culture (1977), his work as a whole has yet to receive broad-scale appreciation outside of Scandinavia.

Naess is founder and past editor of the influential journal *Inquiry* and a past editor of *Synthese*. He is the author of more than four hundred publications in Norwegian, English, German, and

French, nearly thirty of which are books. He has been honored by five festschrifts, one each on the occasions of his seventieth, eightieth, and eighty-second birthdays and two on his eighty-fifth.[14] Naess's philosophizing, as you may well have guessed by now, is by no means confined to the armchair. He is a renowned mountaineer and climber, an occasional nonviolent political activist, and father of the deep ecology movement. His social concern, sense of wonder, and trickster nature have all contributed to his success at numerous academic posts around the world. He is to this day, at nearly ninety, a frequent international speaker.

Arne Dekke Eide Naess was born in Holmenkollen, near the city of Oslo, in 1912. As a child he was fascinated by tiny creatures, shrimp and flies, and he adopted a mountain, Hallingskarvet, as his surrogate father. He studied philosophy, mathematics, and astronomy at the University of Oslo, in Paris, and at the University of Vienna. While in Vienna, he underwent intensive psychoanalysis and trained with Edvard Hitschmann, a noted collaborator of Freud, and enjoyed the friendly, collaborative atmosphere of the famous Schlick Seminar. He received his Ph.D. at twenty-four for his work on science as behavior and went on to perform postdoctoral research at Berkeley in 1937–38 with the pioneering philosophical behaviorist, E. C. Tolman. At Berkeley he went from studying the behavior of rats to studying the behavior of the scientists studying the rats. Upon returning to Oslo, he was appointed to the University of Oslo's chair of philosophy at the age of twenty-seven. He occupied this chair until 1969, when, at the pinnacle of his philosophical career, he sought early retirement to devote himself more fully to ecological issues and activism. Naess has commented that this effort to become more engaged in social conflicts reflects his desire "to live rather than function."

Today, Naess is perhaps best known for his characterization of the "deep, long-range" and "shallow" ecology movements.[15] He views the shallow movement as having a tendency to pursue superficial measures that ultimately fail to address the philosophical, social, and political roots of the ecological crisis. The deep ecology movement stresses the importance of addressing the fundamental roots and coevolving causes of the ecological crisis. It posits that along with humans' special capacities for reason and moral consciousness come special responsibilities, particularly in relation to the flourishing of nonhuman life and the ecocultural sustainability of the planet. The purpose of deep ecology as an ecophilosophical approach is to help people weave descriptive and prescriptive premises about the world, ecological science, and their ultimate beliefs into a cohesive framework for guiding decisions involving society and nature. This emphasis on praxis (responsibility and action) separates deep ecology from the more descriptive inquiries into environmental philosophy that focus on axiological questions, such as whether to extend "rights" to certain nonhumans or how to grade intrinsic value. Naess's work on deep ecology represents the culmination of his effort to integrate reason and emotion. He has created the foundation for a new and promising relationship between human beings and nature, a relationship that positions nature as mentor, measure, and partner rather than servant.

There is no more suitable place to embark on the challenging and rewarding study of Naess's work than the book before you. And there is no finer way to begin to know the enigmatic and inspiring character who is Arne Naess. The better I get to know Naess, and I have been fortunate to work with him intimately as editor of his eleven-volume *Selected Works,* the better I have come to know myself. In a heated debate or tense conflict, I now find myself recalling and working through his "six principles for avoiding misuse of emotions"—avoid irrelevant talk; represent your opponent's viewpoint in the most favorable light possible; do not present a distorted picture that serves one party at the expense of another; and so on. Naess inspires us to stretch, grow, and expand our own potential, perhaps wider than we ever imagined possible. He challenges us to articulate our own total views, to cultivate our own character, but always in a manner that is consistent with our ultimate beliefs and always in a way that does not interfere with the potential for others to do likewise.

I imagine Naess, asked whether the proverbial partially filled glass is half full or half empty, responding, "Both" or "Neither," and then instantly, with a smirk, finishing off the glass. Naess's idea is that by cultivating individual emotional maturity, we grow a wiser, more joyful society, person by person. In this way, phylogenesis might recapitulate ontogenesis. The twenty-first century will undoubtedly be crazy and tumultuous and full of challenges. The more I work through Naess's writings, the more I find myself becoming open-minded and optimistic. I find myself better able to take on the challenges before me with grace and equanimity, and I see myself responding in positive ways to counteract the numbing effects of contemporary society. May Naess's words and wisdom inspire you similarly. As Kant instructed us more than two centuries ago, and Horace before him, more than a millennium ago, "*Sapere aude!*" (Have courage to use your own reason!).[16]

NOTES

1. For a favorable discussion of simulacra as replacements for "real" nature, which requires water, sun, and nourishment, and, perhaps, necessitates human restraint, see Martin Krieger, "What's Wrong with Plastic Trees?" *Science* 179 (1973): 446–55. For a critique of Krieger, see Laurence H. Tribe, "Ways Not to Think about Plastic Trees: New Foundations for Environmental Law," *Yale Law Journal* 83 (1974): 1315–19, 1325–27, 1329–32, 1341–46.

2. E. F. Schumacher, *Small Is Beautiful: Economics As If People Mattered* (New York: Harper and Row, 1973), 85–86.

3. For insight into the origins of Naess's early aversion to emotion, see David Rothenberg, *Is It Painful to Think? Conversations with Arne Naess* (Minneapolis: University of Minnesota Press, 1993), 6–8.

4. For Naess's work on the meanings of truth, see, for instance: Arne Naess, "Common Sense and Truth," *Theoria* 4 (1938): 39–58; Arne Naess, *"Truth" As Conceived by Those Who Are Not Professional Philosophers* (Oslo: Jacob Dybwad, 1938); and Arne Naess, *An Empirical Study of the Expressions "True," "Perfectly Certain," and "Extremely Probable"* (Oslo: Jacob Dybwad, 1953).

For Naess's work on the meanings of democracy, see for instance: Arne Naess, "The Function of Ideological Convictions," in *Tensions That Cause Wars (Common Statement and Individual Papers by a Group of Social Scientists Brought Together by UNESCO)*, ed. H. Cantril (Urbana: University of Illinois Press, 1950), 257–98; Richard McKeon with the assistance of Stein Rokkan, eds., *Democracy in a World of Tensions* (Chicago: University of Chicago Press, 1951) [Naess was the scientific leader of this study even though he is not given credit for editorship]; Arne Naess, Jens Christophersen, and Kjell Kvalø, *Democracy, Ideology, and Objectivity: Studies in the Semantics and Cognitive Analysis of Ideological Controversy* (Oslo and Oxford: Oslo University Press and Basil Blackwell, 1956).

Selections from Naess's work on truth appear in *Selected Papers: Argumentation Theory to Zeteticism, Part 1*, vol. 8 of *Selected Works of Arne Naess*, rev. and ed. Harold Glasser (Dordrecht: Kluwer Academic, forthcomng 2003). Selections from Naess's work on democracy will appear in *Selected Papers: Argumentation Theory to Zeteticism, Part 2*, vol. 9 of *Selected Works of Arne Naess*.

5. For a discussion and elaboration of the positive, inquiring skepticism of Sextus Empiricus based on the work of Pyrrho, see *Scepticism*, vol. 2 of *Selected Works of Arne Naess*. For a more thorough discussion of possibilism and pluralism in the context of the development, review, and ultimate acceptance or dismissal of scientific theories, see *The Pluralist and Possibilist Aspect of the Scientific Enterprise*, vol. 4 of *Selected Works of Arne Naess*.

6. The eleven-volume *Selected Works of Arne Naess* includes the following, in addition to the four volumes cited in nn. 4 and 5 above: vol. 1, *Interpretation and Preciseness: A Contribution to the Theory of Communicative Action;* vol. 3, *Which World Is the Real World?;* vol. 5, *Gandhi and Group Conflict: An Exploration of Satyagraha;* vol. 6, *Communication and Argument;* vol.7, *Freedom, Emotion, and Self-Subsistence: The Structure of a*

Central Part of Spinoza's Ethics; vol. 10, *Selected Papers: Deep Ecology;* and vol. 11, *Stone's Philosopher: Dialogues with Arne Naess on Deep Ecology and Philosophy.*

7. Marston Bates and Philip S. Humphrey, eds., *The Darwin Reader* (New York: Charles Scribner's Sons, 1956), 401.

8. For a general discussion of the role of emotions and feelings in creative development, see Robert and Michèle Root-Bernstein, *Sparks of Genius: The Thirteen Thinking Tools of the World's Most Creative People* (New York: Houghton Mifflin, 1999), esp. chaps. 1, "Rethinking Thinking," and 15, "Synthesizing." For McClintock's experiences see Evelyn Fox Keller, *A Feeling for the Organism: The Life and Work of Barbara McClintock* (San Francisco: W. H. Freeman, 1983); for Lorenz's experiences see Konrad Lorenz in collaboration with Michael Martys and Angelika Tipler, *Here Am I— Where Are You? The Behavior of the Greylag Goose,* trans. Robert D. Martin (New York: Harcourt Brace Jovanovich, 1991); for Gauss's experiences see Agnes Arber, *The Mind and the Eye* (Cambridge: Cambridge University Press, 1964); for Wilson's experiences see Edward O. Wilson, *Biophilia: The Human Bond with Other Species* (Cambridge: Harvard University Press, 1984); and for Polanyi's discussion see Michael Polanyi, *Personal Knowledge: Towards a Post-Critical Philosophy* (1958; corrected ed., Chicago: University of Chicago Press, 1962).

9. For Shepard's central work on the general human effort to reject our animal nature and the effect of this attempted rejection on stunting and deforming our psychological development, which resonates with Naess's overall argument in *Life's Philosophy,* see Paul Shepard, *Nature and Madness* (1982; reprint, with a foreword by C. L. Rawlins, Athens: University of Georgia Press, 1998). For Leopold's blending of reason and emotion to address land management, see Aldo Leopold, *A Sand County Almanac and Sketches Here and There* (New York: Oxford University Press, 1949). For Carson's work on DDT and persistent pesticides, see Rachel Carson, *Silent Spring* (Boston: Houghton Mifflin, 1962). For Justice Douglas's work on environmental policy and wilderness protection, see William O. Douglas, *A Wilderness Bill of Rights* (Boston: Little, Brown, 1965). For Colborn's work on endocrine disrupters, see Theo Colborn, Dianne Dumanoski, and John Peterson Myers, *Our Stolen Future* (New York: Plume, 1996). For Soulé's

work on the biodiversity crisis, see Michael E. Soulé, *Conservation Biology: The Science and Scarcity of Diversity* (Sunderland, Mass.: Sinauer Associates, 1986). For Meadows's work on sustainability and the limits to growth, see Donella H. Meadows, Dennis Meadows, and Jørgen Randers, *Beyond the Limits: Confronting Global Collapse, Envisioning a Sustainable Future* (Post Mills, Vt.: Chelsea Green, 1992). For Nabhan and Trimble's work on the central role that exposure to wild nature plays in children's emotional development, see Gary Paul Nabhan and Stephen Trimble, *The Geography of Childhood: Why Children Need Wild Places* (Boston: Beacon Press, 1994). For an insightful discussion of the significant role that activist-scientists have played in key public policy debates, see Joel Primack and Frank von Hippel, *Advice and Dissent: Scientists in the Political Arena* (New York: Basic Books, 1974). For a window into the power of the artful blending of reason and emotion to address one of the central problems of human existence, our relationship to and bonds with nature, see Stephen R. Kellert and E. O. Wilson, eds., *The Biophilia Hypothesis* (Washington, D.C.: Island Press, 1993).

10. See Neil Postman, *Building a Bridge to the Eighteenth Century: How the Past Can Improve Our Future* (New York: Alfred A. Knopf, 1999), for a similar, favorable view on the Enlightment.

11. Naess made the statement in a debate with Alfred Ayer, recorded in *Reflexive Water: The Basic Concerns of Mankind,* ed. Fons Elders (London: Souvenir Press, 1974), 63.

12. Thomas Berry, *The Great Work: Our Way into the Future* (New York: Bell Tower, 1999), ix.

13. Bob Jickling, "Deep Ecology and Education: A Conversation with Arne Naess," *Canadian Journal of Environmental Education* 5 (2000): 56.

14. Seventieth birthday festschrift: Ingemund Gullvåg and Jon Wetlesen, eds., *In Sceptical Wonder: Inquiries into the Philosophy of Arne Naess on the Occasion of His 70th Birthday* (Oslo: Universitetsforlaget, 1982). Eightieth: Alan Drengson, ed., *The Long-Range Deep Ecology Movement and Arne Naess,* special issue of *Trumpeter,* vol. 9 (spring 1992). Eighty-second: Rana P. B. Singh, ed., *Environmental Ethics and the Power of Place: Festschrift to Arne Naess* (Varanasi: National Geographical Journal of India, 1994). Eighty-fifth: Nina Witoszek and Andrew Brennan, eds., *Philosophical Dialogues: Arne Naess and the Progress of Ecophilosophy* (Oslo: Centre for Devel-

opment and the Environment, 1997); Light, Andrew and David Rothenberg, special eds., *Arne Naess's Environmental Thought,* special issue of *Inquiry,* vol. 39 (1996).

15. See Arne Naess, "The Shallow and the Deep, Long-Range Ecology Movement: A Summary," *Inquiry* 16 (1973): 95–100. For an overview of deep ecology, see Harold Glasser, "Deep Ecology," in *International Encyclopedia of Social and Behavioral Sciences,* ed. Neil J. Smelser and Paul B. Bates (Oxford: Pergamon, 2001). For a discussion of deep ecology with its relationship to Naess's earlier philosophical work, see Harold Glasser, "Naess's Deep Ecology Approach and Environmental Policy," *Inquiry* 39 (1996): 157–87, reprinted in *Philosophical Dialogues: Arne Naess and the Progress of Ecophilosophy,* ed. Nina Witoszek and Andrew Brennan (Lanham, Md.: Rowman and Littlefield, 1999).

16. From Immanuel Kant's "What Is Enlightenment," in *Foundations of the Metaphysics of Morals and What Is Enlightenment?* trans. Lewis W. Beck (Indianapolis: Library of Liberal Arts, 1959), 85. Kant is himself quoting Horace (*Epistles* 1.2.40–41: "dimidium facti, qui coepit, habet; sapere aude, / incipe").

Harold Glasser

Life's Philosophy

1 *Life Seen as an Open Landscape*

> *Everything is conceivable, anything can happen. The future is so unformed that it is neither desirable nor indeed possible to produce a cut-and-dried philosophy of life. If it were, we would stagnate. Philosophy begins and ends with wonder— profound wonder. On that account we ought to consider life, indeed our very existence, as a flowing current. And it is the emotions that set a life in motion. Emotions stimulate you on your way through life and provide the impulse for action and changes of attitude.*

Confronting life can be quite brutal. We are flung into it at birth, then flung further in "encounters" that can be everything from the vile to the sublime. There is something fundamentally unjust in the way we are hurled into life. Some people suffer from their first breath to their last, while others seem to float in sublime felicity all the way. But one need not reject life on that account. There is enough pleasure and satisfaction to give life meaning for the majority.

To live is like traveling through a landscape with both easy and broken terrain, light and dark places, all concealing the unexpected. We travel through this landscape on expeditions big and small, continually interacting with others. We cannot move entirely by ourselves, any more than we can always bask in the sun. A vital aspect of the journey is to take time to tarry in the halts along the way, to pull up and absorb life's inherent values: a beautiful sunrise, a loving smile, a touching piece of music, a cloudless sky.

To feel at home in life requires both moving toward a goal and simply being. The possibilities in this landscape are unimaginable, but anything can happen along the way. The journey is undefined. When we are faced with a critical choice of path, there is a vital challenge in listening to reason and emotion at one and the same time. Another challenge is to turn negative feelings in a positive direction, toward a better quality of life and real happiness. This point of view stems from my optimism about humanity's possibility of being a creative vital force on earth.

Activity and Activeness

Feeling at home in life is for me one of many purposes in living. The metaphor of a landscape is intended to simplify reflections on complex questions. The important thing is that the direction I am following corresponds with that which I find significant, based on the deepest underlying principles of my life—friendship and happiness, for example. To feel at home in life requires both the willpower and the desire to participate in it actively. Woe betide him who goes round with the feeling of being a stranger, one who has landed on the wrong planet.

But what does being active mean? Spinoza has taught me to take seriously in my own life an important philosophical distinction between activity and activeness. I associate the word *activity* with physical activity in the first place, but I also think of intense learning, verbal activity, and reasoning where much is evolving. For me, closeness to Nature has unveiled a marked difference between being active in Nature through play and sport on the one hand and, on the other, experiencing Nature in a way that engages us completely as human beings. The latter attitude may well be consistent with physical activity, but more characteristically it is associated with lingering in silence—perhaps without so much as moving a little finger. A word or two, perhaps even a whole stream of thought might occur to one, but it is the pauses and the internal silence that are the hallmarks of this kind of relationship with Nature. From the outside one might not seem to be active, but as a person, one is completely absorbed. One's whole being is in reality activated in such circumstances, but outsiders do not necessarily perceive one to be in a state of activeness. The more usual state, activity, is concerned with that which is external, and we can be involved in all kinds of activity without being in a state of activeness.

For someone who is absorbed—that is, in a state of activeness—in many different aspects of life, the future is so open and undefined that there is simply no question of having a ready-made philosophy. Even if I might articulate aspects of my total view, of which my philosophy of life is only a part, the fact that it is constantly evolving excludes any finished construction. A definitive articulation would simply imply that I am stagnating. For philosophy begins and ends with wondering—profound wondering.

That many people do not quite grasp where I stand might stem from the fact that I feel that both I myself and life itself are a kind of current, not objects floating in a current. I do not step into the river, as the pre-Socratic Greek philosopher Heraclitus saw it. I *am* the river.

I try to consider emotions as a kind of countercurrent in relation to the exaggerated status of "reason," and do so without presenting the one as a contrast to the other. Instead I propose a concept of reason that is different from the ordinary one. For when we talk of a contrast between reason and emotion, we have too narrow a view of both. I can indicate this in the following manner: to an increasing degree, the word *reason* is used for everything that is rational in a more or less limited and superficial perspective. We need to return to a perception that considers something rational and reasonable *only if* it appears to be so in relation to the broadest and deepest norms—those that are considered most essential for the individual and society. If anything is to be rational, considered from this standpoint, it must not conflict with what a human being has adopted in his heart of hearts, both as an individual and a member of society. At this level mature feelings and reason come together. Reason loses its function where there is no motivation, and motivation is absent where there are no feelings either for or against.

Anything May Happen at Any Time!

One of my first philosophical conclusions followed from the passion that I felt for research. Research is an endless, methodical quest with provisional and inconclusive results, because all things more or less hang together: relationism, not relativism. When, as a pupil in high school, I read that there were *errors* in the proofs in Euclid's geometry and that there were an infinite number of geometries, it made a deep impression on me. Despite the convictions of generations of prominent mathematicians that Euclidean deductions were utterly self-evident, the next generation could nonetheless revise everything. My conclusion was that every conclusion is uncertain in principle, exactly like the moves you make in difficult mountain climbing. They may appear absolutely safe, while at the same time it is always possible to fall. This led me to a so-called Pyrrhonic skepticism. Humans are fallible through and through, and they have no *guarantee* that the future will resemble the past. Anything may happen in the future. There is a clear gap between the conviction of the many on the one hand and the truth on the other. Consensus never guarantees truth.

Possibilism—the assumption that the future is in principle completely open, offering unimaginable surprises—is closely related to Pyrrhonic skepticism, an ancient Greek philosophy that maintained that no certain positive knowledge is possible and therefore demanded the suspension of judgment on all propositions. During the 1950s I propounded a greatly simplified definition of the essence of possibilism in these words: "Anything whatsoever can happen at any time." The main point is that there are no guarantees of anything at all in the future, nor are there guarantees that something is more likely to occur than anything else. Even what are called the laws of Nature are based on events in the past. Since the possible variations of the future are so inconceivably many, we are not justified in preparing for a particular breach of a certain law. To the possibilist, on that account, it seems most natural to be a little conservative and believe in the ordinary; that gravitation in the kitchen, for example, will hold tomorrow, as well as today and yesterday. Plates will fall down, not up. On the other hand, it is only imagination that sets limits to what life can become. I am absolutely convinced that I am not dreaming when I say this, but as a possibilist I must accept that there is a possibility that dreaming is exactly what I am doing.

Another of the ideas that are central to my thinking about life I call *pluralism,* which stresses the importance of a subject or a situation in varying perspectives. These two fundamental attitudes, possibilism and pluralism, might exert such an influence on emotions that they are adapted to helping us out of seemingly unalterable circumstances. Once I was climbing alone down a very long, steep, and rugged ridge in the Pyrenees. I had a thirty-meter rope, so that I could rappel down a fifteen-meter overhang and then pull down the rope after me. Then I arrived at an overhang with a vertical drop of about fifteen meters, which I was quite certain was the longest on the route. The ledge on which I landed under the overhang was quite big. I was convinced that there would not be any greater overhangs further down, so I pulled the rope down to the ledge. But then I suddenly saw that the ledge jutted out over a considerably deeper overhang. I was trapped—completely trapped. Above me there was an overhang impossible to climb, and my rope was not long enough to reach down. My reaction to the situation? I said to myself, "Idiot, idiot, idiot!" After about an hour, I agreed with myself that I would not remain sitting passively on the ledge while I slowly starved and thirsted to death. I decided to try climbing up a tiny shallow crack that ran to the right. It petered out, but at that point I saw a crack running upward to the left. I thought it probable that if I started moving along it, I would fall and be killed, but on the other hand I would far rather die that way than remain stuck on the ledge. To cut a long story short, I saved myself! A drastic reminder that there are always possibilities of survival, even if the circumstances seem quite hopeless.

Naturally I must concede that my argumentation for this possibilism—"The future cannot be guaranteed"—applies also to the reasoning itself. It is quite possible that as a proposition it is faulty. Perhaps I ought to phrase it in this way: I have a feeling that anything whatsoever might happen, that there is no reason to limit the possibilities. But I do not think that this absence of limits has particular practical consequences for my decisions. The possible outcomes are quite simply too many to warrant definite changes to my habits.

Possibilism and pluralism are expressions of the fundamental way in which some of us feel life and the world around us. Possibilism is not a result of definite experience or deductions.

The Creative Life in Nature

Cooperation within what I call the deep ecology movement, with which I am still strongly engaged, is compatible with the conflicting philosophical or religious systems of those who support it. The supporters coalesce in one movement in spite of their differences. One thing that they have in common, for instance, is that they feel and believe that all living creatures have their own intrinsic value, that is to say, a value irrespective of the use they might have for mankind. But the supporters base this view on differing basic values. Some are Christians, others Buddhists, yet others Jews, and others without any particular religious background. There is an invaluable pluralism on this level. I call it level one. We need changes in society such that reason and emotion support each other—in other words, not only a change in a technological and economic system, but a change that touches all the fundamental aspects of industrial societies. This is what I mean by a change of "system." Supporters of such a change may be Christian or anti-Christian or agnostic. They might find their inspiration in the philosophy of Spinoza or consider him quite horrible. At this, in a sense, deepest level of our value judgments, there is diversity, luckily, not consensus. The latter would demand regimentation of our intellectual and emotional life.

To go deep means to go right down to assumptions that we support wholeheartedly. Goal-oriented and sensible choice of action is based on a choice of values that is always based on positive feelings. Every supporter of the movement feels and sees the possibilities of changing the course of the world and the ability of each individual to contribute to that end. Gandhi had a profound faith in the greatness of each individual, irrespective of social status, and an equally strong belief in the possibility of awakening that individual to action. That possibility required great confidence. Gandhi sought it by living with his poverty-stricken fellow humans, inviting them to join in a vast nonviolent movement.

The English rulers of India forbade the people to extract salt from the sea, insisting that it be bought from them. Gandhi was convinced that if he persuaded a large number of poor Indians to march with him to the sea, where salt was formed by evaporation, no power on earth could prevent them. And such proved to be the case. It was a revolutionary, positive action—without violence and hatred. The salt march made a great impression on me. It displayed much emotion and reason.

Many people in the deep ecology movement conceive their basic values on grounds of religious feeling and experience. So too did Gandhi and Spinoza, in both of whom I have found inspiration. Nevertheless, I find it difficult to talk about "religious feelings." When I say that I am not a believer, I mean in the everyday usage of the word, which is associated with belonging to a religion with particular articles of faith. I do not have anything like that. In my youth, I was adversely influenced by the form of Christianity rammed down my throat, in particular by the clergyman who prepared me for confirmation. He was so unctuous, with violent movements of the arms raised up towards the heavens. Later, I rejected the dogmatism often found in religious movements, characterized by sentences beginning "Thou shalt . . . !" and "Thou shalt not . . . !" But it is quite correct to say that I have sometimes been called religious or spiritual because I believe that living creatures have an intrinsic worth of their own, and also that there are fundamental intuitions about what is unjust.

I have always been interested in what lies behind words as they are ordinarily used and interpreted. There is a difference between being skeptical about verbalizations and being skeptical about what lies behind them. The words we use to describe religious feelings and experiences often do not manage to capture what we wish to convey. The manner in which we express our feelings in words is guided by conventions and does not easily make us intensely aware of how feelings are *felt*. One may experience one's feelings clearly, that is to say have a sense of what is felt, but be unable to express it properly in words. So too with religious emotions. Many people may feel, without being able to explain it in words, that it is God who is acting in their lives. In that case, what is most important is the emotion, not the words. All this should be qualified by the reservation that the expression "I feel that . . ." may be misleading. What is present is an attitude or inclination unaccompanied by what might be termed a "felt feeling."

The word *God* is so loaded with preconceived ideas that I see no purpose in using it myself, but if I were to do so, I would choose terminology like that adopted by Spinoza. For him God, *Deus,* is "immanent"—not something outside our world. God is constantly creating the world by *being* the creative force in Nature. Living creatures are involved in creation. I am inclined to accept such a concept of God as a single creative force. We also find in the deep ecology movement that everything in life is interrelated.

I do not exclude the possibility that Christian theological principles are true in a certain sense, for instance, the belief in angels. When my time comes, perhaps an angel will come to fetch me. But I would ask some searching questions and examine how the wings were attached before accompanying him.

I constantly return to Spinoza's opinion: "In a state that is not marked by emotion, one makes no progress in anything that is essential to mankind." It is the emotions that make us something we appreciate being. It is the emotions that stimulate us on our way through life. It is not enough to see the possibility of joining a political party. If one wishes to advance, there must be something that appeals, something that feels good. When one comes to an important crossroad, one puts a number of emotionally conditioned questions to oneself and accepts what feels right; in the sense that there is not only an experience of "Yes!" but a *real* experience of "Yes!"

Spinoza can help some of us understand the decisive role that feelings play in life. When I was seventeen, I read Spinoza's *Ethics*. The book had been recommended by Ferdinand Schelderup, a Norwegian Supreme Court judge and a mountaineer, whom I met in the Jotunheimen Range of western Norway. "*You* will like Spinoza," he said. I was inspired by Spinoza's view of human nature or essence: our nature or essence is such that we are pleased at others' pleasure and feel sad about other's sadness. Kindness and love activate our nature; best of all, they activate all aspects of ourselves. From this he derives his expression *active emotions,* which correspond to what we usually call positive feelings. Hatred, arrogance, and envy, all those we call negative emotions, *passivate* our nature—to borrow a term from electronics. Of course it is not unknown to take pleasure in others' misfortunes; that happens when we become prone to submitting to passive (negative) emotions and eventually become their "slaves," in what is perhaps the somewhat misleading terminology of Spinoza.

Some people may say that Spinoza's view of human nature is too optimistic. They maintain that the nature of humans is such that they are equally inclined to do good or evil. I, however, think that it is unfortunate to say that there is anything evil in human nature or essence. From the moment we are born, we are pushed in very different directions. Spinoza does not profess the opinion that humans are essentially good. What he does mean, as I understand him, is that what we call the positive emotions activate human nature and essence, while the negative emotions passivate them. Such passivating emotions might be reactions to resentment, hatred, and other negative emotions to which one might be exposed after birth. It might be a result of being bullied or, to take another example, of living in the shadow of "successful" siblings. The negative emotions may well be intense, but they will never be as *durable* as the positive ones, since they do not activate the person as a whole. By human nature Spinoza does not mean all aspects of a human being but something more basic. This fundamental element rises to the surface in the form of what he calls the voice of *ratio*. The conventional translation of *ratio* is unfortunately "reason." But what we call reason today is enormously different from what the philosophers of the seventeenth century called *ratio*. When we are confronted with a vital choice of action, *ratio* indicates which choice is in accord with human nature or essence. I add the phrase "or essence" because in Spinoza's day, there was still a concept of essential matter, which added a philosophically important tone to that concept of nature.

Spinoza hardly thought that *ratio*, considered as the voice of reason, was audible in the form of sound. We must imagine it more in the nature of what we call the voice of conscience, an *inner voice* that most often communicates through the emotions. According to Spinoza, the nature of humans is such that a choice of action that *ratio* suggests as the right one is a choice based on active emotions rather than passive ones. In this way *ratio* helps us to transform what we call negative emotions into positive ones. The fundamental importance of such a transformation will be discussed later.

To listen to *ratio* is not easy, but its voice is there regardless of whether we are listening or not—at least that is the way that I interpret Spinoza. And we can develop the ability to listen. Even Spinoza must perhaps admit that one reason only a few people consistently follow the voice of *ratio* is that the less one heeds it, the weaker it sounds. Indifference sets in. We become what Spinoza calls slaves of the passive emotions.

Let me give an example. For many people, to live in a state of being in love is of fundamental worth, but that does not mean that we continually live in a condition of love. Sometimes it is difficult not to hate, if not people, then at least dreadful actions like torture, for example. We cannot avoid being overcome by negative emotions and disappointments on our way through life. What Spinoza seems to underline is the difference between emphatic rejection of the actions of some people on the one hand and hatred on the other. Emphatic rejection may lead to a movement to fight torture as a means of action but need not result in hatred of torturers. Spinoza believes in chains of causality, and a torturer may have been gripped by harmful causal factors.

Spinoza views living in friendship as a process of ripening. However strongly we might feel hatred, it does not seize the whole of our being. Love and friendship may do so. *Ratio* helps us to convert hatred into something else. Incidentally, Spinoza puts more faith in friendship than in certain forms of love. Intense love may slip into hatred, especially if it is based on the other person's appearance. This happens more rarely in friendship, since this is governed by clear (albeit unarticulated) rules; the strength of the emotional commitment may diminish from time to time, but it is always *durable*. Now and then Spinoza uses the expression "firm friendship." According to Spinoza, society is based on feelings and attributes of friendship. Nowadays we often use the expression "brotherly love" in a way that, in my view, is related to friendship and friendliness.

The Artificial Gap between Reason and Emotion

In society at large there seems to be a large gap between reason and emotion. On the one hand, we tend to see cold reason; on the other, warm but often uncontrollable and shortsighted emotions. This is an unfortunate situation. Reason, in the sense of Spinoza's *ratio*, is no cold, calculating platitudinous commonplace. The question "Ought I to follow my feelings or my reason?" is simply irrelevant if it becomes a question of which feelings, and without feeling there can be no spur to action. What we need is always to unify feelings and reason in the sense of *ratio*.

Something that makes it difficult to understand what I mean by this here might be that *I* often describe as feelings what others might consider much too weak to be counted as such. But it is an essential point for me that very faint feelings are important in differentiating moods. In the workplace it is relevant to establish the precise mood of one's boss, not only whether that mood is good or bad. In this context, the word *emotion* is inappropriate because it seems best suited to denote fairly strong feelings. "Outbursts of emotion" is more applicable than the expression "outbursts of feelings" or of "moodiness."

As I use the expression "the life of feelings," it stands for something rather more fundamental than anything else we call life, like working life or family life. Faint but highly important feelings are almost always present. A faint prevailing negative feeling may spoil a life and reduce the quality of life of a whole family or professional partnership, sometimes leading to alcoholism or drug abuse.

It follows that in many ways suppressing human emotional life is to suppress human life itself. I find it worrying that someone who is highly developed emotionally in a positive sense—that is to say very mature—is forced to play second fiddle, being valued less than a person who has done something sensational or "useful" to society at large. There is no sense in stipulating either-or: "One either follows reason or submits to one's feelings."

Some people may perhaps be puzzled that I, who have been seen as an exponent of reason, have chosen to devote a whole book to emotional life. People do not realize that for some of us, abstractions are full of exciting mysteries. It is precisely my intense feeling for abstract intellectual activity that has made it so easy for me to decide to write as I do, both now and in the past. My passion for abstract subjects, including mathematical logic, can lead to my doing just as much that is "unreasonable" as someone of a completely different nature. In chemistry, physics, astronomy, and mathematics, I was induced to continue in exactly the same path all the time. I took no pleasure at all in being diligent and making sure that there was a kind of progression, as required by my studies.

By and large, it is painful to think.

At the same time it is obvious that people with a leaning toward the abstract may have too easy a path to responsible positions in our society. And those who find pleasure in abstract subjects are often more prone than others to face difficulties in family life and other social relations. There have been remarkably few family men among the great philosophers. Among other things, this might be because they have somewhat short tempers. They can be distant, living in another world. For that reason they are rarely interested in politics and do not become "dangerous" as thinkers. Socrates' wife, Xanthippe, had a hard time. She is often unfairly treated as a nag. But Socrates could be difficult to live with.

When I was twenty-seven, I had the choice of two university chairs, although emotionally I was still in my teens. But since I always had so much entertaining whimsy to offer, I could acquire good, loyal friends without really pulling myself together.

The logical empiricists of the Vienna Circle, with whom I had many discussions in 1934 and 1935, clearly argued from a logical point of view, but with passion. And they were involved in politics of a radical kind. They felt that dominant German philosophy served political reactionaries and the Nazis. Heidegger was a frightening example to them. They wanted to replace traditional philosophy with a "scientific" view of the world or with "logical premises." For my part, I took seriously both the system of Spinoza as a profound confession of philosophical faith and the doubts of the American thinker William James that abstract logic could be used in philosophy. One of the logical empiricists agreed with me about the latter. What I greatly admired among the logical empiricists was their determination to argue in an unbiased manner, even in the most impassioned debates. There was an unusual atmosphere of goodwill at their meetings, which I had never experienced before and rarely since.

The French philosopher, mathematician, and natural scientist Blaise Pascal said in a well-known passage, "The heart has its own logic, which reason does not understand." And in everyday life one often hears people say, "I ought to have listened to my heart; it was right." Faint but significant feelings, positive but occasionally negative, accompany our decisions. Arguments for or against are mostly just registered, not "felt," but sometimes a conclusion is deeply emotional and said to "come from the heart." Looking back, the choice is in a direction that led me to applaud the function of reason. Nothing should be called reasonable that does not support one's basic values. In critical situations we may safely offer seemingly contradictory advice: "Follow your reason and let your emotion decide; and follow your emotion, that is, let reason *(ratio)* decide."

The point here is that *ratio* and the positive feelings coalesce in an internal relationship deep in our being. An external relationship occurs when there is no particular context in life, and reason and emotions do not lead us in similar directions. But to assert that emotions are reasonable in themselves, or that reason has emotions in itself, is to make things paradoxical. Reason and emotions function in different domains. Emotions may be a source of good sense, an inspiration to insight, wisdom, and meaning, but they might also lead to the diametric opposite.

Pascal's dictum reminds us that we can be completely surprised by an emotional reaction to particular circumstances: "This morning I was certain that I would like . . . but I disliked. . . . This afternoon I was certain that I would dislike . . . but actually I liked . . ." Some people find the unpredictability enjoyable and believe that it reinforces the feelings of self, that is to say, the feeling of being something that has the power to go its own way and has enough confidence to do the unexpected. The judgment of the heart can be quite unfathomable. Time-consuming, perhaps unhealthy, egocentric, observation can uncover more and more of our own emotional reactions in their interplay with decisions.

Emotions are not objects, things that we own. They emerge from an encounter between ourselves-and-the-world. I use hyphens as a reminder that a sharp distinction cannot be drawn between ourselves and the world. And it is not the case that we merely *have* emotions, any more than we *have* relationships. We *are* emotions and relationships. We cannot stand outside ourselves. In a broad sense, those thoughts, emotions, and relationships with which we identify are, in other words, a part of ourselves. The transient feelings that we have for a bus driver, for example, depend on whether we consider him or her as a subject—that is to say a fellow human being—or as an object, a part of the bus which is conveying us where we want to go. Recent philosophical discussions focus on the difference between the "I-thou" relations and the "I-it" relation. There is a suspicion that the big, affluent industrial societies are fostering the latter. We tend not to feel others as fellow human beings perfectly on a par with ourselves.

Positive feelings may grow out of a meeting with a bus driver— perhaps the person in question greets us with a smile—or they may follow as a result of a general positive state of feeling we are in before we enter and leave the bus. This may sound complicated, and so it should, since, as human beings, we are almost incomprehensibly complex, interesting, and original, even in our so-called simple functions. It is only if we do something of either trivial or great social and legal significance—for example, if we commit a murder—that the spotlight is switched to the events of a moment in ourselves, and therefore in our tangled relationships.

Sometimes a friend seems to have fallen victim to chaotic impulses, confusion, erratic argumentation. In such circumstances it may be particularly suitable to urge the use of reason. The question must be asked, "What can be done now? What plan of action is the best for you, under these particular circumstances in this phase of your life?" And in this case it is vital that emotions and reason (in the sense of *ratio*) must be seen in the context of the fundamental values on which we base our lives. To see a deplorable conflict between reason and emotion may be due to a poor understanding of the situation. It is Spinoza in particular who, in my view, has given us the concepts and a greater possibility of avoiding this trap.

The Playful Human Being and the One at Play

It is not my job to describe emotions in particular circumstances, but to reflect on them at a fairly abstract level. At a critical juncture motivation, and therefore feelings, drive us to action and changes of attitude. But the concept of reason that I use is such that reason is always needed when we have to judge which emotion activates us at a particular moment. It reminds us of other emotions that ought also to be taken into account, and it judges the results the next moment or at some other time in the future. Normally all this happens with little verbalization, but suddenly there comes a point where we have to try to talk to ourselves or to others.

That prestige which I myself have gained for my contribution to abstract thought is, without doubt, appreciably greater than that which would have resulted if, instead, I had devoted myself to developing a mature and noble emotional life. In the latter case it might have been said of me: "Don't you know Naess? A mature and noble person—but he never became anything." As it is, though, my foothold in abstract subjects has led to my "becoming someone." Although I have managed to preserve my humility toward my work, other people, and life itself, I have never felt that life was hard or that I was inadequate—mainly because I had an extremely good start in life; I loved someone who I thought was my mother, and I was loved. I have always had a strong but not exaggerated faith in myself—a faint but positive feeling in thinking that I am someone who counts, at least as a family member. Nonetheless, it was never unpleasant to discover that there were those who were more competent and some who were much better human beings. Wounding remarks on the part of opponents left no scars. To that extent I have been a lucky devil. Such basic self-esteem and self-respect are a solid foundation on which to build.

When I was about five years old, collecting big numbers meant a great deal to me. I obtained a lot of notepaper and wrote down all the big numbers that I came across. I had particularly pleasant feelings for the numbers on railway goods wagons. It was a true pleasure in abstract things and not in cars, for instance. This collector's pleasure was perhaps somewhat dampened when I heard that there were infinitely many numbers. Consequently there was no point in writing them all down.

Some children develop strong feelings for the fantastic and gigantic. And this brings me to teaching. I want wonder to be emphasized more in all education, and what is "certain" to be put more in the background. There is a connection, although a somewhat loose one, among big numbers, big waves, big intervals of time, big distances to the stars, and great goals and affairs. But at the same time we must encourage children to seek the great in the small, a feeling for greatness coupled with a feeling for the tiny, tiny little pleasures, little ripples on the water.

I believe more seriously than many others that it is beneficial as an adult to preserve the childlike, imaginative wonder about life. Children have a less defined, fuzzier attitude to the divide between reality and imagination, a divide that plays a decisive role among adults. If parents were to participate in imaginative wondering, the imaginative powers of their children would survive their school days better. But the parents would have to make it clear that they do not describe facts.

Letting one's imagination run riot should not impede the process of maturing. The same condition applies to what I would call "artists of life"—a *lebenskünstler*, to use a German word, someone adept at the art of living, who is driven by playful emotions. And without humor and play it is easy to lose the spark required to do something about the great worldwide problems. It is remarkable how some people who are or were deeply involved in desperate, serious matters, such as the Dalai Lama and Gandhi, always have a smile waiting to break out. Without that, they would scarcely have managed to continue their work.

By reflecting on emotions and philosophy, I am trying to make more people reflect creatively on their opportunities in life—focusing on feelings rather than on what is conventionally called reason. I find it remarkable and unacceptable that the matters that I raise in this book are discussed very little in academic philosophy. When I talk about such things in university lecture rooms, people evince great attention, almost gratitude. Among most people there is a constant discussion about emotions and their particular roles, good or bad, in conflicts big and small, but rarely about emotions in general and in the context of a philosophy of life. I am trying to convince people that the development and maturity of feelings are just as socially important as the development and maturity of knowledge, and that they must be furthered in schools and universities. This educational program demands serious public discussion. I hope that this book, together with many more on related subjects, will contribute to the relevant changes.

But as I have said, it is often difficult to express in words what we wish to convey. I am concerned that people express themselves clearly and precisely about emotions and their philosophy of life to avoid misunderstanding, which may cause conflict and unnecessary bad feelings. An approach to life that seems dogmatic on account of the way that thought is put into words can cause confusion and stop discussions that may reveal new viewpoints and perspectives. Strangely enough, my experience supports a belief that training in formal logic and unbiased verbal communication is not a threat but an aid to attempts to change schools and universities in the direction of the development and maturity of feelings.

2 *How Do You Feel Yourself and the World?*

*We ought to ask more often how we feel ourselves and the
world. The fact is that the division between ourselves and
the world is not clear. It may be troublesome to put feelings
into words, but to suppress them rarely leads to anything
fruitful. Our emotional life seems so rich that it is almost
impossible to grasp. Are feelings subjective or objective? And
how can we distinguish between true and false emotions?
At the same time, feelings have a far from unequivocally
positive status in our society, fixated as it is on intelligence.*

Someone has just come on a visit, bringing mail with him. I
found a card from a friend on which was written, "How do you feel
yourself and the world?"

The question was well put. Today people need to concentrate
more on *feeling* the world. It ought to be natural to ask the question
my friend asked. Why not! Because emotions have such a low status
in our society, people say, "This is how I see the world," or "This is
how I understand the world." They do not say, "This is how I feel
myself and my situation." Emotions are undervalued in our deal-
ings with life—in spite of their central role in practically all social
and private contexts. Can something be done about it? I believe that
it can.

I like to sit at the living room window of my isolated mountain
hut, Tvergastein, which offers an eagle's eye view of the very Nor-

wegian scenery of the Hardangervidda Plateau. It is easy to let my thoughts soar far away. Here, there are no distractions like radio and TV, no sounds except the wind. Above all, I have a work space that I have built in the southwest corner with a view over untrammeled space, a precipice of the majestic Hallingskarvet Massif as my closest neighbor, and more than fifty thousand square miles of landscape within sight.

Up here it is difficult not to think big. Polemics and gossip become impossible. Here we tread warily in the landscape of both place and thought. I find it difficult to understand how Nietzsche could manage to write pettifogging letters among the high mountains. Perhaps I have not read those letters carefully enough. I hope that those who have done so, and call them less than elevating, have judged wrongly.

At Tvergastein, I find serenity within me, a serenity that the Hallingskarvet Massif also seems to possess. Bitter blast and hurricane, snow and rain—nothing can disturb its serenity. I recall a phrase from my favorite philosopher, Spinoza: *acquiescentia in se ipso,* "a serenity within oneself." That kind of serenity does not prevent the wind from blowing strongly in life. But it is an inner consolidation and presence that means that in every kind of situation one can feel like a complete human being. I feel that kind of serenity only in the way of life here at Tvergastein. Nature seems to help us to find that kind of calm. Some seek the mountains, others the sea, and still others the forest.

I feel a particular affinity with the small animals up here. As a three-year-old, and later, I was together with tiny shrimps and flounders off the beach at Norheimsund in western Norway. I was so much bigger than they, but if I stood still, they might suddenly turn round in midflight and inquisitively examine me. The flounders sought shelter under the soles of my feet. I took that as a sign of confidence. Then and there I unquestionably developed a sense of being part of a vast world of living beings. When I was five years old, my family bought a hut at Ustaoset, on the Oslo–Bergen railway. At an early age I felt that inner serenity when the steam engine hauling the train puffed from Geilo over the tree line to Ustaoset Station, where we had a fairy-tale-like view of the Hallingskarvet. Gradually the naked rock face became like a faithful old friend—a divine dream of a father figure.

When I built the Tvergastein hut in 1937, my wish was to live in the high mountains. I did not want merely to come on visits but to become someone who belonged there. All in all, I have now spent about twelve years of my life up here. So when I am asked how I feel myself, I can say that it is here that I feel myself completely, without reservations; and I feel it best of all together with a good friend or my wife—someone who talks little and gets up late, so that I can be together with the place early in the morning. I do not make a very clear distinction between myself and the hut and the vegetation, especially the flowers. I feel well when the place is in bloom.

Up here, five buckets of water in midwinter make you rich. All essential needs are satisfied, I can have many different experiences, and there is enough to occupy me; in short, I have a rich life. To reduce wealth to money and possessions is an incredible underestimation of our emotional life. Some of the wholeness that I feel up here is already lost on the train journey down to the city with its fuss and demands. Then it is good to try to take an inner serenity with one.

Everything becomes more alive here. A blue towel from 1937 is riddled with holes, but it has served me for more than half a century and has become something like a living thing. Since there is never any hurry here, objects have plenty of opportunity to talk to me. Those people are wrong who believe that I am particularly sensitive up here. It is merely that the surroundings, and the objects contained within them, speak so much more clearly. I really do believe that little by little most people, at least here in Norway, would consider vegetation, minerals, and kitchen utensils in a different light, if they would only make the time to be at a place like Tvergastein for a little while. They would themselves become receptive beings, with different moods in the course of the day. Some people might perhaps say that I am projecting emotions *into* the surroundings. In other words, I am projecting something within me and attaching it in one way or another to a tree or something else in my surroundings. However, I believe that it is more correct to say that the contrast between me and what is not me changes. I become more a part of the surroundings, and the surroundings more a part of me. What remains is a network of more or less intimate relations. I call this relationism.

When my friend asks how I feel the world, it is an intricate question. Does he mean *my* world or the wider world? I assume that it is a combination of the two. The short answer is that the world participates in that which I feel, and the other way about. The world and I are not that far apart, perhaps not even by so much as a millimeter. I have no very clear idea what are the limits of the self; perhaps it flows out and expands, or contracts within. It is never the same. It seems more like a *flow* than anything solid. Is the diversity of feelings that I register only within myself, as if in a kind of box? Is consciousness like some sort of a container with pictures of *external* things? That seems nonsensical to me, like an alienation of the world out there and a degradation of the great flow of consciousness.

This has gone on far too long. But perhaps it will give a picture of the infinite multiplicity of emotions that we have time to dwell on during our lives, and which we can leave undisturbed in its twisting and turning and disguises and playful fancies at Tvergastein.

The Varied Expressions of Emotional Life

Is it difficult to express emotions? This peculiar question can be a good point of departure for reflection. In self-preservation, any strong culture will define a framework for what people ought to feel and how they ought to express their feelings, if at all. This often makes people avoid giving honest expression to their emotions. Whether we find the framework strict or mild, we must face the fact that for many people, suppressing emotions can lead to depression and other conditions that are anything but desirable.

Clinical psychology and psychiatry reveal much of the difficulty that quite a number of people have in expressing their emotions. Words are not enough. For all I know, perhaps most of us have an emotional life just as complex as that of Franz Kafka. But almost none of us can put emotions and experiences into words like he did, even though we all have our own unique way of expressing ourselves. In different groups in society, there may be different conventions for which verbal expressions ought to be used for particular emotions. Many emotions are not "in"; others may be virtually prescribed.

If one goes to psychoanalysis in its original form, one usually hears repeated exhortations of the following kind: "Say precisely what occurs to you!" and "Don't hide anything that you feel!" In 1934, when I was undergoing psychoanalysis, I interpreted such exhortations as a cognitive theoretician and as an academic philosopher with analytical training. I was specially trained in what the French philosopher Henri Bergson calls *les donnes immediates de la conscience,* conventionally translated as "the immediate data of consciousness." During the first few days the analysis situation became more and more embarrassing. About ten times more occurred to me than I managed to express—and at least ten times as many different shades of feeling passed through my mind. The experience of analysis was complicated in itself, and while I was saying something, a voice within me was talking *about* the talk. Six days a week for fourteen months, I went for analysis to the experienced Freudian Eduard Hitschmann. How did he manage to interpret my flow of speech? Remarkably self-controlled. At the end of the first week he announced, "I can say with certainty that you are not a schizophrenic."

When we talk about our own and others' emotions, we usually have limited aims—we merely chat. To that extent, small talk is a good expression. I would guess that most people would regard with horror the possibility of everything they say in the course of a week being published in thick leather-bound tomes. It would be even worse if we included everything that passed through a person's head, not to mention all the emotions and thoughts. However, what is surprising is that a great deal in such an imaginary leather-bound volume would bear witness to the enormously rich imagination of mankind. For a few short moments imagination rules in an admirable way, but without our even consciously observing it.

Just as I was writing "a few short moments," I stopped writing and looked slightly to my left. There was a little saucepan of water radiating good cheer. A spoon lying across the lid seemed for a moment like a broad, smiling mouth, but then turned into an independent object quickly on its way to the right. To me, the ability to analyze the experiences of the moment is a source of wonder: wonder at human creativity and approval of the result of evolution during hundreds of millions of years. That which happens within us—in our minds and hearts—is so complicated that the psychoanalytical instruction to express everything that occurs to one becomes quite simply an exhortation to do the impossible.

The Difficulties in Expressing What We Feel

Let us imagine that we are walking over a hilltop and enter a new landscape. At first—in less than a second—we may have a clear feeling, but before the second has passed, it has vanished. We might perhaps have expected to see something completely different, so we were presumably disappointed. Two ingredients were most discernible, the feelings of surprise and disappointment. But there were perhaps more components—relief, for example, that one had finally reached the top of the hill. We have all known occasions when we were seized by the moment, and the simple dimensions of time and space vanish. It is difficult to put such moments into words. Saint

Augustine's little aside has become famous: "If you ask me what is time, I am unable to say, but I know what time is." I am tempted to adapt him: "Ask me what I felt, and I am unable to say; but I know what it was."

I remember an intense personal experience that concerns the relation between emotions and the consciousness of expressing those emotions. It was connected with French lessons in high school. I was generally miserable in school at the time, being interested in subjects other than those being taught. I chose classics, because I believed that to be the easiest way to get through high school, but it turned out to be a mistake. I was completely uninterested. My aim was *just about* to pass my examinations. But there was always something in existence in which I was deeply interested, and then all "subjects" were completely irrelevant. I felt really sorry for my French teacher. He turned a blind eye to the fact that I was obviously learning practically nothing. It would have been his duty quite simply to fail me. Kind soul that he was, however, he disliked the thought and sent me to the headmaster to apprise me of the situation. Herr Rokseth amiably asked me if I would promise to pull myself together so that at least I would avoid failing. I thought for a few seconds before answering, not with a forthright yes but with a forthright no.

Whereupon the unforgettable happened. The headmaster reacted with the following words: "You agree with Luther that the way to hell is paved with good intentions?" I was completely speechless, but the headmaster rose sky-high in my estimation. It was a fantastic, friendly interpretation of my uncompromising, impolite no. No more was said, at least that I can remember, but it annoys me— I almost feel tears in my eyes at the thought—that I was not mature enough to say a few words, not just the bare, negative no but with a few words that expressed what I was really feeling. I ought to have said something like: "My French teacher has done all that he could to make me learn a little French. His patience and tolerance of my behavior has been amazing." And then I would have said to the headmaster, "And that you, Sir, answered my no with a quotation from Luther was fantastic. Clearly you disagree with my opinion, that one cannot promise anything in a world where anything may happen?" That was the way that I myself felt—hence my answer to his question—but I could not bring myself to express something I would have liked to have said in addition to a mere no. Now it is too late.

This example is a reminder of the difference between strong, emphatic emotions on the one hand, and enduring albeit not intense feelings on the other. The distaste at not being able to say what I ought to have said turned out to be enduring. It will last until I die.

That experience of mine is also of some interest for the unending inquiry into the relation between guilt and regret. Today there is perhaps a tendency to regret rather than feel guilty. Maybe we learn more about our possibilities: "I could have done so and so . . ."

To What Extent Can We Distinguish One Emotion from Another?

No two people have had exactly the same emotions during a given interval of time. Emotions, thoughts, and sensations form an uncharted diversity that will always vary from one person to another, even in the course of a minute. In addition, new emotions are constantly arising. There is always something new under the sun. If we say that a thousand children in a parade seem to have precisely the same feeling of joy, and a thousand other children have also felt joy, but not of the same kind—what then do we consider the nature of the similarities and differences?

It is perhaps even more difficult to give an answer if we are dealing with a feeling of boredom. If we believe that two people have precisely the same feeling of boredom, which symptoms particularly come to our notice? And precisely how is boredom experienced? Is a multiplicity of emotional differences actually felt, independent of descriptions of people and situations, for instance? To take an example:

> A: I had to listen to him for a whole hour. I began to be bored.
> B: Was that all you felt?
> A: No, I had a little cramp where I was sitting.

In this case A acknowledges that he experienced boredom, but if B had said, "Did you not feel anything?" A might have answered, "No. Oh that's not quite true, my stern was a little sore." Perhaps we ought to consider boredom as a special feeling, or then again perhaps not.

My conclusion is that the diversity of feelings is immensely rich. Some would say that there are few that are "really" different. So which characteristics do we use in deciding that one feeling is different from another? An important question: Are we to include no references to a particular situation or more general circumstances in which A and B are acting? On the contrary, in this case it is essential to give a description of and references to the situation and context in which A and B are acting. The felt emotion may very well be the same but appear to be something quite different in another situation.

To take an example: homesickness, the urge to travel, the longing for freedom—are these different feelings? Ought we not perhaps to admit that in this case we are dealing with what is fundamentally a single emotion—longing—and that there are many varieties of one and the same emotion? But is that to be understood? Varieties of an emotion must be emotions. They must be felt differently—or so one might think. But ordinary ways of talking do not consistently function in that way. In the way that I use sentences of the type "X is a feeling that I have," we must freely acknowledge that he who utters the sentence might be wrong. Thus: "For a long time I thought that I was fond of Therese, but unfortunately I turned out to be wrong." And again: "When I was in Nicaragua, I felt very homesick, or so I thought. But when I returned home, I grasped that I was really longing for something quite different, which was to see Christine." When you read fiction, you will come across many descriptions of the multifaceted phenomenon of longing and understand how subtle and polymorphous the field is.

The multiformity of our emotional life is no illusion. But there is a strain in the philosophy of emotion which wants to limit this multiformity to a mere two basic feelings, namely, pleasure and pain—a positive and a negative feeling, two feelings which admittedly vary in the intensity of their factual content. Such a reduction of the world of feelings can easily lead to undervaluing emotional life by comparison with the intellectual. "Emotions? They are simply variants of desire and revulsion. And that is what we have in common with animals." Acknowledgment of A is completely different from that of B. A textbook may contain a thousand alleged declarations of differing certainty and range. In my view there is good reason to trust everyday speech and that which it expresses: we meet the different circumstances of life with a rich variety of felt emotions. We can always try to group, classify, and arrange, but I believe that it is unlikely that one day a Linnaeus of the emotions will be born, someone able to describe phyla, species, families, and orders of felt emotions in a wholly comprehensive and convincing manner. There is little to suggest, luckily one might say, that emotions *allow* themselves to be classified as variants, subspecies, species, and so on.

These are many words about words. Among other things, this is due to the ambiguity of words, to the fact that they can be given a variety of different, reasonable interpretations. Even in serious research into passions, emotions, feelings, and moods, it is necessary to take into account that words that function satisfactorily or reasonably well in daily life give rise to fruitless discussion among savants if attention is not paid to the richness of meanings or usages of everyday words. By a clear and fairly unambiguous definition of the meaning of a word in a discussion, it is largely possible to avoid apparent agreement and disagreement that are only due to ambiguity. It is futile to ask who among the theoreticians in sociology and philosophy use certain words associated with emotional life correctly, and who are wrong in the sense of what the words "really" mean. For that reason it is also futile to talk about words as if they were concepts. Rather we may say of a word that it *expresses* a concept.

What then about words used in discussing emotional life? There are those who believe that when they use the word *emotion* they are using it synonymously with *passion*. Others declare that they use *passion* only when applied to something that is clearly associated with the body, senses, and instincts. They say that deep professions of friendship based on passion can, for example, easily arise in a state of intoxication. A tendency to be friend or foe increases with alcohol intake. But such passions last only for a short time and do not have consequences for emotional life as they conceive it. In short, when asked about words characterizing the world of feelings, people have formulated many hypotheses.

To have a feeling of friendship toward someone is something different from a feeling of passion, although occasionally some would characterize a friendship as passionate. Some will say that they use the words *sensation* and *feeling* synonymously, while others declare that they use *sensation* only if they can localize it physically, like toothache for example. One has sensations in a particular place. Spiritual suffering also has analogous physical effects. But in the use of the expression *sensation,* it seems that there is little point in adding, "But perhaps I am wrong." If I say that I have toothache, I might have to enter a correction after having been to the dentist: "Unfortunately, it is the jaw." But in that case some people might add that the sensation was the same. If John says, "I have an unpleasant feeling that something might happen to us," he would undoubtedly be puzzled if we ask, "Where do you have the feeling?" In this case the connection with place and anatomy is hardly relevant. But even if John says, "I have an unpleasant sensation that . . . ," he may not consider it pertinent to be able to locate it.

Emotion is a word that I personally do not use. It is often used as a synonym for *feelings,* but it is too obviously associated with intense feelings to be a close equivalent of what I mean by feelings. This association becomes more evident when we look more closely at the word *emotional.* Some people are said to be more emotional than others, the word often being used pejoratively. The same applies to the adjective *sensitive,* albeit to a lesser degree. Later in this book, I will investigate more closely what I characterize as extremely faint touches of feeling. In that context the word *emotion* is hardly suitable; it is better adapted to feelings that are quite intense, feelings that move one. "You say that you don't feel anything when you are sitting there. But I believe that now you have emotions as well." In this case it is more appropriate to assert that the person is feeling something, albeit very faint, unnoticed by most people. A "tone of feeling" is present. It is rather like saying that after a sunset a red tone still remained on the horizon, or that an answer had a tone of reproach. Some people, on striking a key on the piano, can also hear the overtones, clearly but faintly.

Closely related to what I have been talking about is a question, somewhat more doubtful or profound: Can we *describe* feelings *themselves,* and can we describe the differences? Or are we simply recognizing something without description, as if pointing to an object?

"I felt abandoned."

"Yes, I understand how you felt."

Has the first speaker thereby described the sense of abandonment itself? We can hardly say so. We may describe a piece of apparatus that we have never had but wish to have. If we obtain it, we might perhaps put it on a table and examine it more closely, together with someone else. It is different in the case of feelings. Admittedly there are articles and books that describe and characterize different kinds of pain, for example, gripe or distension in the stomach. But perhaps we cannot describe a feeling that another creature has unless we ourselves have had such a feeling. It is difficult enough even if we have actually felt it.

In a group to which I belonged as a teenager, we used to talk about something we called "organ sensation" when we felt nothing. We might have detected a kind of faint, positive message from our body, a message that could not be called a definite feeling and came from the body rather than from the spirit. Organ sensations occur when we are waiting for something, a bus, let us say, or something else that will soon come but is not awaited with any particular anticipation. We *simply* wait. But if we are in a situation where something is horrible or wonderful, it is quite simply impossible to sit and wait for a bus in that way. Some people often seem to have a sensation of impatience, a sensation of unrest that is negative, while others only have rather weak but positive sensation of simply existing, let us say, of just being.

The point of view I wanted to clarify here is that the feelings we have when we are inclined to say that we don't feel anything characterize our positive or negative attitudes to life. It might mean, for example, either that one is suffering a mild form of depression or going round and feeling a faint degree of pleasure.

The Prevailing Tone in Emotional Life—and Other Tones

Let us examine more closely those situations in life where we consider "Nothing!" to be the appropriate answer when we are asked what we feel. In such cases it may nonetheless be said that one does feel something—incredibly faint perhaps, but something nonetheless. I interpret this something as a weak *prevailing tone* in our emotional life, be it positive or negative—a prevailing emotional tone. It is a faint feeling, pleasant or less so. An observer can *see* such a feeling when, for example, it results in a slight curling of the corners of the mouth, either upward or downward. The longer students remain at a university, the more often one can see a tendency for the corners of the mouth and the look in the eyes to be dragged down. This is really bad. Unquestionably it is a result, not of natural causes, as among older people, but quite simply of boredom and stress. To talk about happiness or despondency is to go too far. A prevailing tone in their emotional life, what I call the prevailing emotional tone, is something that underlies emotional life, something that is there for long periods, whether we are aware of it or not.

I am referring to the sensation that one has when one does not feel anything quite distinctly. The faint negative alternative may be indicated not only by the word *emptiness,* but by a new expression: one has a feeling of *being lived* rather than *living.* One carries on with the daily routine but not choosing to do so with a clear positive or negative feeling. One becomes a kind of living automaton. The prevailing tone that colors one's life depends on circumstances. As a student, while within the university precincts, for example, one might have a faint negative prevailing tone—a minor key, as it were—while at home one's tone is faint positive—a major key—and a smile comes readily.

I distinguish a prevailing emotional tone from an emotional tone that changes from moment to moment. There is a basic mood and a fluctuating one that changes from time to time. The relation between prevailing tone and tone is similar to the relation between the layers of wax on the bottom of a ski. The prevailing tone is like the foundation waxing, and the tone like the succeeding layers of wax required by the particular snow conditions. It is the foundation wax that provides adhesion for the other waxes. In the same way we can say that emotional life plays on an infinitely rich variation of emotional tones, but by and large it is characterized by a single prevailing emotional tone, which may be good or not.

Let us imagine that we are at an important but long-drawn-out meeting. First something interesting is said, then something banal. Now and then we laugh a little; at other times we smother a yawn. I admire those people who have the ability to maintain a positive facial expression, albeit a faint one, during the periods when nothing seems to be happening. At moments such as these, others, perhaps most of us, feel impatient, restless, or otherwise very faintly negative. If I interpret the circumstances correctly, although a few participants will have a positive prevailing sensory feeling, however long the meeting, most will have a negative one.

By comparison to the prevailing emotional tone, which is long-lasting, individual emotional tones are short-lived. People often resort to the mountains or the sea in search of a positive emotional tone. This may be one of intense positive anticipation. But then something unexpected happens along the way. Perhaps the weather in the mountains is not as expected, and we are deprived of the chance of sunning ourselves. Instead, a crossword puzzle awaits us indoors. The emotional tone can change into something negative, to disappointment. But the reverse may happen. Children who have been dreading a boring holiday might perhaps find new friends and discover that a stay in the mountains is the best thing that could possibly happen to them.

It is relatively easy to change a particular emotional tone from negative to positive. It is far more difficult to change the prevailing emotional tone itself. A remark like the following is based on the prevailing tone: "Since you moved here, you seem a little depressed. We must do something about it." The person thus addressed may have had paroxysms of laughter several times without making the remark less valid. In certain situations it might happen that a particular emotional tone manages to change a prevailing tone. Perhaps one might meet someone attractive while waiting at a bus stop and fall in love. That produces an intense positive emotional tone and can change the negative prevailing tone. To what extent the intense feeling is transient or long-lived is difficult to say. There is no guarantee that, in spite of its intensity, the infatuation will be long-lasting. Love and hatred can be particularly durable emotions.

Thus our emotional state is characterized both by a prevailing tone and a series of detached tones. For longer or shorter periods people seem to have a settled positive or negative prevailing tone. The expression "It is good to be alive" expresses a positive prevailing tone. Perhaps it is easier to express the prevailing tone when it is negative, as in the case of persistent worry or emptiness. In that case the answer to the question "What do you feel?" can be the same: "Nothing." Note that here I am not thinking of circumstances where in fact we are clearly thinking of a settled pain or pleasure. "How are you?" can elicit the response, "Not so well."

"Then what's the matter?"

"Nothing really."

But the answer can also be, "Very well, thank you." The question "How are you?" is rarely an invitation to probe deeply.

The expression *emotional tonality* is only distantly related to tonality of speech. But in certain circumstances it is said of someone that he is speaking quite tonelessly. To take an example: John is telling James that a dear friend of both, who has long been mortally ill, is dead. The feeling of emptiness that can then arise can result in toneless speech, in emotional exhaustion. All strength of feeling seems to have vanished.

When we set ourselves the task of surveying different feelings, it is useful to distinguish between their intensity on the one hand and their strength on the other. I think it is tempting to talk about the durability of feelings—their immutability and permanence, combined with the capacity to assert themselves when several different feelings seem to compete in attracting one's attention and deciding one's course of action. The intensity of a feeling may be such that it continually demands attention. Less intense feelings can easily be neglected.

A long, successful expedition—whether in the mountains or in life—requires invincible feelings of friendship and, in addition, a constant feeling for the mountains or the goal of the expedition. The deeper that positive or negative feelings are anchored in one's emotional life, the more they are attached to what I call durable feelings. I call an emotion durable in relation to circumstances in which it is put to the test. Illuminating examples:

> "That's the umpteenth time that his left ski has loosened, but he is just as happy with the trip!"
> "She has called him a shit every day now, but he is just as keen."
> "It has been forty-five years since she had an affair with someone else, but he is just as indignant at the thought of what happened."

Light and Dark Temperament

The emotional state that characterizes us during various happenings in life depends on the prevailing tone on the one hand and, on the other, on the many strong tones in our emotional life. The German language has the word *Stimmung* for that which we call emotional state. When we talk about the dark and the light temperament, there is one aspect that we may also call the emotional state. We thereby touch on a divide that in my view is philosophically and psychologically vital, namely, the difference between a light and dark temperament. It says a great deal about someone if one of these terms can justifiably be applied to that person. The familiar saying "The glass is half full" hints at an attitude that may be said to characterize the way in which the light temperament regards events. To use the metaphor of landscape, we can say that the light temperament will more easily see the happy features—an exultant waterfall, a smiling stream. On the other hand, "the glass is half empty" characterizes the dark temperament. It does not deliberately look for anything negative in the circumstances. On the contrary, for such a person the negative aspects spontaneously stand out above all else and must simply be accepted as such. The light temperament not only guarantees a preponderance of the positive prevailing tone but also, within certain limits, pleasure and contentment at whatever happens. The motto "Think positive!" has unquestionably had a good effect for many people. To a certain degree it can be seen as an admonition to seek consciously for something good in situations that at first sight seem completely dark—that is to say, to achieve by a conscious attitude that which the light temperament manages of its own accord.

On the basis of what we have hitherto considered, we may say that an emotional tone will be present in every situation except a dreamless sleep. But what about circumstances where nothing seems to make any difference? In Greek philosophy, under these conditions, the word *adiaphora* plays an important part. The basic meaning of *diaphora* is "difference," and *adiaphora* therefore can be applied to something that makes no difference. In a more specialized and limited sense, it is used about matters that, according to a philosopher, ought not to make any difference to life, something insignificant. For other people the same concerns might be decisive, but for a real philosopher? Dross, philosophical *adiaphora!*

Nonetheless, we must consider situations of indifference and unconcern in everyday life. It is necessary to analyze the feeling of unconcern. It is a fairly general phenomenon in a thoroughgoing welfare state. If one is poor, practical matters of survival continually arise. These are obviously important, and long-term considerations are put aside. Things are different in a state of affluence. There are many who fight their little daily battles against apathy. I have heard some people say that they are "ready to do practically anything to get rid of apathy." To some people nothing seems worth their attention. "When I wake up, I have the feeling that nothing whatsoever has any meaning. What am I to do with yet another day? What shall I do with myself? Everything is meaningless." The completely apathetic person seems to have lost the power of emotional commitment to any significant degree. Any initiative beyond the most elementary kind is out of reach, nor is it attempted. It is difficult for the completely apathetic person to be anything but a burden to his surroundings and society at large. Compared to other characteristics, such apathy is regarded as detestable. One must pull oneself together and get rid of it! Some manage it on their own, but for the majority outside help is of incalculable worth. It is a positive experience just to be together with someone else who believes that something or other is worth attention.

If apathy persists, the philosophically inclined will have a tendency to assume generally pessimistic, nihilistic, or cynical points of view. "There is nothing wrong with me; the blame lies with you. You don't understand the emptiness in existence." On the other hand, the philosophical twist can enable a completely apathetic person to carry on with a reasonably good quality of life. He is pleased with his insight, but even under such circumstances attacks of desperation are not unknown. Quality of life is concerned exclusively with how one feels about oneself and the world.

Do Ethical Values Exist Objectively or Only Subjectively?

In this and the next sections, what appear to be rather elementary remarks are made. They actually concern matters of great importance for all of us, and I find it justifiable to remind the reader about them. They deserve some reflection.

Philosophically, there are grounds for distinguishing between the *feeling* that something is unjust and that something *is* unjust. Injustice may be conceived as a reality, irrespective of emotion. Some people will say, "Such-and-such is unjust, and it's not merely something that I feel," while others might protest, "No, it is either something that *you* feel, or part of your cultural 'constructs.'" This distinction has led to deep discussions and attempts at clarifications, but there is no ultimate agreement. Consensus within a group is often a sign of an absence of concern with fundamental aspects of society.

Some theories of emotion in ethics deny realism, the doctrine that something simply *is* unjust. Put very simply, such theories of emotion postulate that there is no real or inherent justice or injustice independent of felt justice or injustice. Much is clearly a matter of emotion.

For my part, I am a realist or absolutist in ethics. Nazism has provided examples of what I consider to be unequivocal and obvious injustice. But the motivation to do something about it, the motivation to bother about it at all, does not merely require a negative judgment and negative emotional reactions. Unjust treatment may be observed with total passivity. A psychopath may learn about right and wrong but lacks the inner motivation to do what is right and reject what is wrong. This may partly be said to derive from a complete absence of emotional engagement in questions of right and wrong. "What is the point of such a distinction? It doesn't matter to me."

What about those things to which one is not indifferent, which set one afire, and which make a difference to life? To take an example, the details and goal of a walking tour might be determined by features in a landscape: a beautiful hillock, a mountain summit, a charming rivulet; things that stand out a little, grab our attention, and help us to find our way. There is a telling German word, *Merkwelt*, for which the closest English equivalent is "everything that a definite being is aware of." Anyone who takes a dog for a walk notices how it smells everything! The dog perceives itself as walking through a scentscape and not a landscape. There are naturally other things beside scents, but scents are enough to make the walk delightful. The dog's *Merkwelt* is largely different from ours.

If you walk together with someone along a road, you will observe fairly distinct differences. Some people consistently observe many more and different things than most others do. We can say that they have a richer *Merkwelt*. Usually they observe something with positive feelings, but sometimes with disgust or other negative feelings, like boredom. In this case, what I propose to call the repetition problem is involved at full strength. "But it's one and the same thing," "I've already seen it so often," "I can't cope with it again." Ronald Reagan, the former American president, is alleged once to have said of the majestic redwood trees on the Pacific coast of the United States something like "If you've seen one, you've seen them all." So why not keep on felling trees when there are so many of them, each one like the other? Some always see "the same" where others see the difference. Consider this exchange:

Anne: You're always going on the same walk!

Beatrice: No, I never go on the same walk!

Anne: Why are you staring out of the window? They're only boring clouds.

Beatrice: They're never the same clouds. They're always new, always worth looking at.

To some people there is an almost inconceivable variety of things worth attention. We ought to let these people help us keep the ability to take pleasure in things and events that reveal themselves to us. If one is depressed, the *Merkwelt* is much reduced. Those who work professionally with people of extremely low IQ report that much which is trivial to us appears extraordinary to them. A door that opens and closes automatically becomes a source of wonder.

The False and the Genuine in Emotional Life

We are often told that emotions can get us in a muddle, that they sweep over us, that they are subjective and not to be depended on. The question we can ask ourselves is to what degree emotions are genuine. Some will say that all emotions are genuine in the sense that they *are* present. One who feels ill really does have a feeling of being sick. But suppose someone then says that one is a hypochondriac, and one agrees. After a few repetitions, the person who just now felt sick will call the same feeling something different, a "strange feeling," for example. Whatever the conclusion, the feeling was really there.

In my view some sensation was present. However, if one classifies the emotional state as some specific, labeled feeling, one might be mistaken.

An encounter with a large beast of prey can arouse an instant response, positive or negative, depending on what we are bearing in the form of preconceived ideas and assumptions, partly unconscious, about beasts of prey. Many people will have a feeling of fright, but an animal photographer, for example, will have feelings of keenness and satisfaction. Yet others will perhaps experience pleasure mixed with fear. If we attempt to describe what passes through us in the course of even so short an interval as three seconds, the outcome cannot be anything other than more or less hypothetical emotional classifications.

Is it reasonable to maintain that we more or less mistake our emotions in everyday life? We can say so if it is a question of trying to determine those emotions with absolute certainty or acquiring a complete understanding of them. This is obvious in the case of complex emotions in a complicated situation, when social and cultural influences are also involved.

In this connection, perhaps we ought to accept that no description of emotions in a particular situation can be definitive. Perceptions are changeable. As with all other historical material, it is possible to reevaluate the matter. The many false sources in the writing of history are precisely dealt with in historical methodology and the philosophy of history. Catholic and Protestant descriptions of the prosecution of Galileo have always been different. Emotionally conditioned conflicts never seem to acquire any definitive description. Family feuds offer good examples. The conflicts may peter out, each party changing stance a little: "I never meant . . . ," "I only meant that . . ." More interesting are concessions: "I was not really as angry as I seemed." Only rarely does a slight misinterpretation of our emotions lead to conflicts and unpleasantness. We say rather that "the others" have a somewhat twisted or a not wholly realistic concept of what they are feeling, but we don't make a fuss about it. "I can't bear going through all that again."

The question of genuineness in our emotional life is an issue of more or less daily importance in the sense that according to unwritten social laws, particular emotions ought to apply to certain kinds of situations. If that is the case, one ought adroitly to express feelings that one often does not have. "Thank you so much for the tie; it is quite wonderful." In point of fact, the tie evokes a feeling of revulsion—something so gruesome is a rarity, one thinks. Moreover, faint but distinct feelings of distaste may arise, because now one is obliged to reciprocate by giving a present in return. What is more, the expression "thank you" was false, because at that moment one received the impression that the donor merely wanted to get rid of the tie. In this case, we can talk of a complex series of expressions of false emotions. Politeness constantly prescribes a number of modest deceits of this nature. Literary authors are much superior to us poor philosophers in describing what is false and what is genuine in emotional life. False emotions are a leading subject in the professional literature on emotion, and it is unlikely that I have anything new to say on the subject. I merely wish to pursue some philosophical aspects of the matter.

There are those who maintain, with some justification, that normally we go around wearing a mask and give expression to something that does not exist behind the mask. When it finally dawns on a little child that she is being watched, her natural reaction appears to be shyness. The formation of the mask is beginning. "What I really think and feel I will keep to myself." But it seems as if some people never have the feeling of being observed. They may easily give a slightly vacant impression when engaged in concentrated thought. The Danish physicist Niels Bohr seems to me a good example. When he discussed profoundly fundamental problems and wrote formulas on the blackboard, his lower jaw occasionally dropped down somewhat. He quite simply stood agape. We others, without knowing it, are perhaps more like actors. Our appearance is not unimportant to us, although we are not conscious of it and may even deny it. It is a great thing to be able to behave like Niels Bohr—and not a few others—who from their earliest years have been consumed by interests and causes they feel to be far greater than themselves.

Philosophy enters when we consider questions of whether we must or ought to seek "genuineness" in different senses. If the answer is yes, how high a priority ought genuineness to have? It is said of some people that one can always depend on the genuineness of what they say that they are feeling. But there is a temptation to call them naive. If they are caught in exaggerating or understating the strength of what they are feeling, or if they do not have an honest conception of which feelings are actually present, is this to be interpreted as a personal defeat? The answer is not to be found in psychology. That requires articulated and emotionally colored value judgments. Nor is it purely and simply a matter of ethics.

One example of a conflict in relation to the genuineness of emotion is when someone says, "I am fond of you." Our hypotheses of how fond we are of someone else, of the depth of our undoubtedly warm feelings, are of great importance in everyday life. Is true love what we really feel? What distinguishes *to be fond of* from *to love*? In many circles during the twenties and thirties, if Arnold and Beatrice were in love or besotted with each other, considerable responsibility was involved in saying, "I am fond of you," and gazing into the eyes of the other party. If Arnold, a young man, dared to hint that he had an affair with Beatrice in mind, the formulation of the answer could be quite decisive: "I don't know if I am fond of you," for example. That meant an unequivocal no. A declaration on Arnold's part—"I am fond of you"—had to be an expression of a *genuine* emotion with far-reaching implications of clear, lasting, strong, 100 percent positive emotions. The temptation to utter exaggerated expressions of devotion was great. On the other hand, engagements were not infrequently broken, and the consequences for the injured party could be disastrous.

The existentialists, particularly Jean-Paul Sartre, often made genuineness and falsity a subject of their thinking. In his last work Sartre branded himself a traitor—not least a traitor in regard to his own emotions. The title of the text—*Les mots (The Words)*—hints at this. When language appeared, lying arose, and a huge increase in the opportunities for lying, dishonor, and falsity. When a passionate discussion descends into quarreling, it often ends with one party saying, "You won, but I'm right." Because eloquence is unevenly distributed, the remark is, sadly, often justified. The losers are frequently embittered by such experiences, and the victors, made arrogant. According to the Bible, "Blessed are the poor in spirit, for theirs is the kingdom of heaven." Even if a simple soul talks perhaps as much as anyone else, his linguistic abilities are more modest, and that helps!

Be Reasonably Sensitive, and You Will Live Long in the Land

Many people who consider themselves to have a good life ask themselves: "What is the good life?" Here I use the expression "the good life" ironically, for it actually sounds as if a particular kind of life is the good one. That is naturally not the case. The path to the good life goes primarily through the emotions. Only secondarily does it go through the apparatus of reason.

Let us look more closely at the status of emotion in a society of our kind. It often seems as if the answer to the question, "How are you feeling today?" is concerned with our state of health: "Not so well, I am coughing a little." The qualities emphasized in obituaries are often concerned with a highly developed and mature emotional life, but it is a *little* late to acknowledge this in an obituary.

What earns recognition in society is production, in other words, what we have "achieved" in the course of a life. At the same time, much of what we appreciate within ourselves and in others is connected with something different, with emotional life in fact. The word *sensitivity,* which ought to evoke unequivocally favorable associations, is often associated by society with hypersensitivity, emotionalism, being thin-skinned, and other qualities of a negative kind. If we compare *very sensitive* with hard-bitten, many are those who will place the latter higher. Have pity on those who are sensitive.

It is disturbing to consider how low a status is accorded to the emotions in contemporary society. They are dismissed as something that takes us by surprise and ought more or less to be put aside. Such overpowering and demanding conventions naturally have an effect on *which* feelings put their stamp on our emotional life. Today we often find people who, for long periods of time, are slaves of negative states of emotion, like apathy, angst, and aggressive impulses.

It is hardly surprising that when one who hears me say that emotions are undervalued in our society will protest: "What do you mean? Society is full of sentimentality and emotionalism. Take advertising, for example: it generally appeals only to our emotions." True enough, but usually a few, simple emotions. A catch phrase like "a rich life with simple means" might seem quite useless to a marketing specialist. On the other hand, I would not be surprised if it were to be used in the near future, albeit to market something rather less complicated.

What Does "Becoming Something" in Society Imply?

Not infrequently one hears judgments like "But he never became anything." As late as the 1930s in the Norwegian class system, to become something was closely connected with the social class to which one claimed to belong. Manual workers and skilled craftsmen became something if they had honest work. Among the upper or lower middle classes, it was unthinkable for parents to see things in that way. To be a goldsmith or practice a similar craft was acceptable, but preferably combined with owning one's own business.

The distinctions were emotionally loaded to a high degree. The subject "becoming something" deserves to be considered in the light of emotional perspective. The opinion that a certain occupation was unworthy often had no particular justification. It was self-evident.

Emotional life can be such that it slows the pursuit of higher education and better status. All Norwegian municipalities have recently been meticulously classified according to their standard of education. Baerum, an affluent suburb of Oslo, unquestionably leads in this league. In one of the "worst" municipalities, in northern Norway, the answer was as follows: "The occupations of most of us in our municipalities are such that we need experience rather than formal education." A sober and excellent reply! Without justifying it at this point, I would go so far as to say that a highly developed and mature emotional life might easily lead to weak motivation in "getting on."

A few examples have made a deep impression on me. I think of someone who died without becoming anyone, as the saying goes. He was very fond of flowers and of growing vegetables in the family's garden. Eventually he specialized in the shades of color in the blue wood anemone. He knew everything about this flower and was in a position to talk about it authoritatively. But naturally he did not have enough of that form of knowledge required to pass an examination in botany. He did not become a botanist. He liked singing and listening to others sing. But he did not practice systematically. He did not manage to become a professional singer. He loved the theater and tried to become an actor, but was not sufficiently convincing. He did not drive himself in the way that was needed. In other words, he was a gem of a human being, a wonderful source of pleasure. He performed countless services, but since he did so absolutely without payment, they were not included in the gross national product. There is much talk in our society about encouraging the creation of values, but is that what we really mean? What kind of values? Increased humanity does not count, but a huge increase in the sale of electric toothbrushes really affects the gross national product.

I have another example of becoming someone from the many years that I used to arrive at my office in the Philosophical Institute at the University of Oslo around half past six in the morning. I would meet a cleaner in her forties. The more I talked to her, the more she seemed to be what I would now call emotionally highly developed and mature. When the 1968 "revolution" broke out, the students were given their own room for their many meetings (not mine, I hasten to add, as the press reported then and now). The cleaner became desperate, talking about coffee stains and other marks on the floor—in other words, the room was a mess beyond description. She said that it took just as long to clean that one room as whole floors of the building. I suggested that she ought to leave that particular room alone. No one would reproach her. But she insisted on continuing the work, partly because she saw it as her duty and partly because she quite simply could not bear to see a room in that condition. I mentioned this to a student who was so radical that he considered the local Stalinist faction of the Communist Party to be petit bourgeois. It was therefore not surprising that he also thought that the cleaner was being petite bourgeoise in feeling obliged to clean up. I might be wrong, but that cleaner seemed considerably more developed and mature emotionally than either the student or I.

We ought to learn not only to accept people who do not "become anything," as it is defined in society, but to show enormous *gratitude,* indeed admiration. The fact is that someone can become somebody in the sense of being a human being—and become someone very great. Kierkegaard has pointed out how important it is simply to be a human being. It means developing humanity in the deepest sense of the word, and that implies maturity in emotional life.

It is striking, in my view, that those people who have so many opportunities but do not seize them often show greater emotional maturity than those who seize all. Some are counted as lazy or without initiative; others do not seem to understand how to get on, how to use their ability and how to take advantage of their opportunities.

In such cases it is obvious that in the main, ability and opportunity are regarded as means to achieve that which is conventionally seen as being successful, with signs of success judged by society's narrowest definitions.

Intelligence Gone Astray

The rich industrial countries are characterized by choosing relatively superficial qualities as signs of what are called reason and intelligence. It is only to be expected that in our times we put a high value on knowledge and intellectual ability. Our unique position among living creatures on Earth depends far more obviously on our intellectual capacity than on anything else. Often ironically, we call our species *Homo sapiens*. It is ironic because the Latin word *sapiens* means "thinking" or "understanding" and is concerned with intelligence and wisdom. Theory and practice must go hand in hand. But those who are intelligent do not have a reputation for also being particularly understanding or wise. Rather, they are shrewd. Shrewdness has a remarkably high status by comparison with wisdom. Perhaps there is much uncertainty about what wisdom actually implies. To me, wisdom implies taking a long view, a sense of priority, a high degree of reflection.

Next to shrewdness, intelligence has a high status. The word is derived from the Latin verb *intellegere* and noun *intellectus*. One Latin dictionary mentions the following suggestive meanings of the verb: "to understand, divine, to be a judge of, observe, feel, think, imagine, mean by, understand by." Our use of the word *intelligence* reveals an extremely far-reaching and, in my view, unfortunate development in parallel with the development of society. Since the seventeenth century we have separated emotions from what we call the intellect. Intelligent people are precise and logical. But there is another word: *understanding*. We say that A might be extremely intelligent but lacks understanding. Understanding people, we admit, can hardly be unintelligent but need not be more than moderately intelligent. The word *understand* has obvious connotations of feeling in many of its main meanings. To take two examples: "She had great understanding for Tom's attitude in this affair" and "He has no understanding of her difficulties."

Mentally retarded people with low intelligence, as the word is defined nowadays in our society, may be normally or very well developed emotionally. On the other hand, those who seem emotionally underdeveloped or immature may manage very well in the so-called IQ tests. These have very little to do with understanding. Does not skill in dealing with other people depend on having an understanding of the emotions of those others? And does this capacity for understanding not play a greater role in one's own progress at work than does skill in solving problems, as intelligence tests attempt to measure? I belong to those who would answer yes a priori.

And then what about the recently discussed "emotional intelligence," EQ? In his book *Emotional Intelligence: Why It Can Matter More than IQ* (1995), Daniel Goleman has a practical aim, as the subtitle suggests. This aim is partly to replace intelligence tests with something else. Goleman believes that to raise the level of social and emotional ability among children, "the schooling of emotions" should be given the same weight as improving the acquisition of technical knowledge. Goleman's initiative is extremely valuable. But any replacement of the concepts of intelligence with EQ ideas will scarcely be considered, given the way that our society is organized. If similar methods are used to measure EQ and IQ, one might easily wonder if we are not reverting to the same ancient dualist system that separates the cognitive (rational) and the conative (emotional). But under any circumstances, the EQ "movement" ought to be warmly welcomed.

The standards of society often emphasize the rate of "progress," in the sense of initiative in subjects that appeal to the intelligence. Concentrating on emotional intelligence, in Goleman's sense, is an attempt to introduce another measurement besides that which is assumed to demand intelligence. This is particularly important in deciding how well suited someone is to a job—"social intelligence," as it has long been called. One must be able to interpret the body language of one's colleagues, besides having the capacity to work both independently and together with others. One must also show consideration for others and have the ability and desire to practice the basic forms of brotherly love.

To stigmatize the EQ movement as an expression of antiintellectualism, as has happened, is misleading and unjust. The attempt to focus attention on the role of feeling and emotion in life always merits a closer study, but in practice, taking it to greater lengths naturally hides many traps. One such trap for teachers of EQ can be to teach people to be *shrewd* by increasing the knowledge of and attention to what other people are feeling. A good tactician with a high EQ is equipped with social antennae, which means that he can hold a large gathering or a small group in the hollow of his hand.

My main object in this chapter has been to shift many issues from a purely psychological, sociological, or ethical treatment to one based on philosophy and the management of the emotions. Above all, I have tried to bring to the fore certain priorities that have simply been undervalued or remain unarticulated. Schools and universities give little guidance here. Young people are burning with feelings and opinions of fundamental worth. They may become burdened with a feeling of helplessness because they cannot manage to explain what they stand for.

Even if there is no open conflict, it is worthwhile to present the rich spectrum of different value systems and revel in the fact that such a variety exists: "Oh well, you have a diametrically different point of view from mine in this question. That's encouraging."

3 On Imagination, Research—
and Petty Rationality

In science and philosophy the logical and not the emotional man has been the focal point. The rationality that characterizes the knowledge society is of an extremely limited kind—a petty rationality—that does not ask what are our most fundamental priorities and values as human beings. This rationality has lost sight of our aims and is merely concerned with means. Is the conflict between emotion and rationality real? And is it not often imagination and emotion that drives scientists and scholars?

If we survey the philosophical landscape, we see an inner relation between what I will now call the philosophy of emotion and the different components of a philosophical conspectus or system—logic, general methodology, cognitive theory, ontology, value theory, descriptive ethics, prescriptive ethics, philosophy of science, political philosophy, social philosophy, and aesthetics.

In Western philosophy human beings are primarily seen as cognitive creatures. Thought has a unique position in the life of *Homo sapiens*. In philosophy we have been far more impressed by our highly developed knowledge than by our standards and quality of emotional life. Theory of knowledge and of cognition, in a wide sense of the term, has posed a long series of questions, to which widely differing answers have been given for approximately twenty-five hundred years. As a matter of course, professional philosophy, with its thousands of practitioners, has occasionally dealt with fundamental issues concerning the emotions. Compared with other philosophical subjects there is nonetheless not much to be found in books and articles on this theme. It is virtually the equivalent of how things stand in everyday speech. We do not have many negative expressions about cognition, but a fairly large number where emotions are concerned. For example, we say, "It's only a feeling," or "Keep feelings out of it." "To become excitable" is a common expression, but not "to become cognitive." "She is very sensitive" is not usually a compliment.

Theory of knowledge is one of the main parts of philosophy. But does emotional theory also have a valid claim to the same standing? In any case, theory of knowledge has had indirect consequences for everyday life, and emotional theory might have a similar effect. It is almost trivial to maintain that strong feelings may play a part in deciding one's philosophical view of life—even if that view is presented without systematically explaining and accepting the function of emotions. What I ask myself is whether we philosophers might *alternate* between expressing ourselves as cognitive and as emotional creatures. Like the fundamentally emotional creatures that we are, we might, for example, be more inclined to say things like "I feel that x is closer to the truth than y," "As I feel the world, it is like this . . . ," "As I feel myself, I am like this. . . ." Might philosophers not put more emphasis on discovering at which points emotions appear in the succession of thoughts? We ought occasionally to permit ourselves to say, without reluctance or awkward excuses, "Well—at that point I was affected by the feeling that . . ." To which a critic might reply, "I feel this in quite another way," and then proceed to describe how he felt about the matter. Naturally, the next step will be to search for reasons and causes why in this particular instance feelings were so different or led to something so different.

According to one's upbringing or position in society, there is a greater or lesser tendency to say, "I feel that . . . ," or "The way I feel about . . ." But such statements often seem defensive: "I maintained *x* but admit that I only felt that way. . . ." In judging for or against, and in evaluating the particular consequences, one person will appear to rely on cognition (insights, facts) more or less exclusively, while someone else will maintain that, strictly speaking, that person is talking "only" about feelings.

One reason for the comparatively low standing that emotions are still accorded in society at large is that people ascribe to them little or no value as knowledge. Despite opposition, society gives a higher priority to polishing the technical and knowledge-gathering abilities of people. Even in the environmental movement, it is said that those who support a technocratic-economic rationality are too full of emotion. In other words, they are seen as being driven by emotions and not intelligence. The existence of such attitudes, both in society and in philosophy, proves how technologizing has stamped the educational system. It implies a false appreciation of the true and essential role of emotions. We might well ask to what extent philosophy and psychology in particular have contributed to the low cognitive standing of everything connected with emotional life.

Even if there is such a negative attitude toward action based on emotions, there is just as marked a negative view of lacking feeling. But deeper feelings like sympathy and empathy have to be turned on or off according to need. Violent outbursts might be almost acceptable occasionally; strong feelings are not quite as good; sentimentality is really dangerous. A worker with great integrity can be dangerous. You simply cannot ask: Why are we producing this? How are the production processes and their uses related to that which we think is significant in life? What are the consequences of this production for other people's lives and other living creatures?

One of the most important things that I am trying to say in this book is that we ought to talk about how we feel about things, ourselves, and the world, more often and without qualms.

Reason and Rationality on the Throne—Petty Rationality

I would warn against allowing the continually rising flow of information and knowledge to dominate as the foundation for our decisions and judgments. But what about the high standing of reason and rationality in philosophy? Does this mean that we cannot trust the emotions and must depend on reason? Or is it the other way about? There is much talk today about the transition to the knowledge society, where cognition and reason are given pride of place. Or we are told that we must put feelings aside in public debate. Strong feelings might impede the rational, the scientific, and the "most objective" view. Feelings are seen as coming over us, as something over which we have no control, while we can depend on understanding. That which understanding bringeth forth must of course necessarily lead to sensible, balanced, and correct decisions.

But by this I mean that by and large it is a question of trite reason or what I prefer to call petty rationality. Those decisions are reasonable only when judged from an extremely narrow perspective, but they are wholly unreasonable, or at best neutral, when considered in the light of the broadest and deepest human values—when we ask ourselves what is most important in our lives.

Perspective has many dimensions. The two simplest are time and space. We repair something in a way that is good enough for a day, but we know that the repair will probably have to be repeated in a week. Or, on the other hand, we may carry out a more comprehensive and time-consuming repair that we estimate will last for three months. Another example: we take an excellent but uncertain and temporary job that is satisfactory seen from a short-term point of view, but what of the long-term factors? Ought I to buy an apartment on the assumption that I can keep this particular job? Whether something is reasonable always depends on precisely what kind of time perspective one adopts on the basis of "given" facts.

The simplest kind of transition from a narrow to a broader perspective concerns precisely this time perspective. What is the best policy for fertilizers, seen in the light of this year's crop and next year's yield? What is best over the next fifteen years? What is the best thing to do with radioactive waste products in the short term, and what ought we to do if the period is a hundred years? A contentious question is, What is best for poor, unemployed Brazilians in the big cities? Ought the authorities to give them areas in the rain forest that they can cultivate—or try to improve their circumstances where they are living? Considered in the short term, the first alternative seems superior. On the other hand, if we take account of the fact that the soil in the rain forest does not lend itself to cultivation in the long term, then taking the longer view suggests improving their situation where they are.

What is called rational argument is given a high standing in debates, but what is rationality? In this case an extension of perspective is also called for. Fundamental goals are more important than rationality in isolation. One example that I often use is parking for private cars in a city center. A parking lot may be eminently sensible in the way that it is placed and built. The plot has been cleared and prepared according to all the best tenets of engineering, with the use of sophisticated machinery and a particular kind of surfacing. On the assumption that a parking lot in the center ought to be precisely there, this one is perfect. But ought it to be there at all? The conclusion is no. Building the parking lot in the city center shows a complete lack of foresight. It ought to have been put in a completely different kind of place. And that was really a consideration when the need for a new parking lot was mooted. But another consideration was quickly forgotten, which was that private motor traffic ought to be banned from city centers. Why? We have underlying or more profound aims with which city traffic conflicts. These aims have in their turn even deeper ones. We are dealing here with a chain of relations between means and ends that must be discussed in a broad perspective. If something is reasonable or rational within a perspective P_1 but unreasonable or irrational according to a broader perspective P_2, the conclusion must be that it is both unreasonable and irrational. Generally speaking, perhaps we ought not to describe anything as sensible or rational if it is irrational in relation to our deepest concerns. I propose that we change our use of the words *reasonable* and *rational* in this direction.

In philosophical discussions emotions are often presented as competing with rationality. I am more concerned with the kind of irrationality that is often without more ado characterized as rational or shrewd. And by irrational I mean, among other things, that which happens when someone underestimates the emotional side of a question. Perhaps we start off now and then with the chimera that we are faced with a problem of pure reason, only to admit afterwards that in reality it was decided by powerful emotional forces. This is what I wish to put under the spotlight—not to undermine trust in reason, but rather to investigate how reason and feeling actually work together in many situations in life.

Six Rules for Objectivity, against Misuse of Emotions

In the cultural conflicts within the industrialized states, the fight against what we call "objectivity" is important. Here it is vital to tread warily. A revealing expression is "to turn something into an object." In German *Verdinglichung*—"converting to a thing"—has been an essential term, particularly in neo-Marxism. To see human beings as objects, and to approach a person in this way, is inconsistent with true human fellowship.

In my view we ought to avoid the words *objective* and *objectification*, because they have such a wide and disturbing variety of meaning. There is, however *one* meaning of the word *objectivity* that concerns a fundamentally positive phenomenon. It is not a universal truth that is sought in what is objective but a form of impartiality that we attain when we follow the six ethical rules of verbal communication. I have chosen to call these "the principles of avoiding undue bias." They may be broadly summarized as follows:

1. Avoid irrelevant talk.
2. In a serious discussion, any formulation aimed at representing the opponent's views must be such that the opponent considers the representation to be adequate.
3. Any argumentation ought not to suffer from ambivalence of the kind that leads listeners or readers to interpret the opponent's statements in an unfavorable way.
4. Do not ascribe to opponents opinions that they do not profess. Do not argue with imaginary or contrived opponents.
5. A presentation ought to avoid giving the listener or reader a distorted picture that serves the interests of one party at the expense of others.
6. Context or outside circumstances that do not concern the subject ought to be kept neutral.

In such a highly condensed form, the six norms seem to say more or less the same thing, but if we consider some concrete examples, the differences between them emerge clearly. The norms have this in common: that they protect an opponent against unfairness. The expressions "objective descriptions" and "to look at the matter objectively" often stand for "unbiased descriptions" or "to look impartially." Of course we must retain and develop the six rules of avoiding bias in communication in conflicts. But the phrase "objective descriptions" ought to be banned. Neutrality, on the other hand, as *I* wish to present it, concerns how we represent the opinions and factual conditions of others.

A vital component of Hitler's battle is often described as a battle against objectivity. In that case the word stands for impartiality.

Germans had to stop being objective in the sense of impartial. "Think with your blood!" And when the blood was boiling, it was easy to accept biased propositions, about the character, mentality, influence, and aims of the Jews, for example. The strong, ever-present emotional intensity of Hitler's rhetoric was critical for his victory in the 1930s. Hitler's and Goebbels's ministry of propaganda perfected the art of generating and exploiting negative emotions. The victory of Nazism depended on people becoming what Spinoza called "slaves of the passive emotions"—first and foremost the hatred which the Nazis managed to arouse.

The Chinese leader Mao Tse-tung took the campaign against the rules of avoiding bias a step further. In the last phase of his regime, it was illegal to quote the opponents, or rather those who had been branded as opponents of the regime. They could be reported only in indirect speech so that suitable insults or denigratory expressions could be inserted. For example, in English translations of a political opponent's views, the report might begin with a phrase like "He trumpeted that . . ." instead of the more neutral "He said that . . ."

Music Conveys Emotions Better Than Words Do

To many people music releases such intense and lasting impressions that a discussion of the subject must naturally be a part of my philosophizing on emotional life. In the history of Western music, the romanticism of the nineteenth century made an unambiguous and direct appeal to the emotions. This gave rise to some friendly, tolerant, or absolutely negative criticism, even if that criticism was not directed toward composers like Chopin and Brahms. Accusations of sentimentality were often leveled against music. The critics declared, probably with justification, that they could observe falsity in the very expressions of emotion. To take one example, for some years—from the 1930s onward in any case—the Russian composer and pianist Rachmaninov was accused by musical experts of sentimentality. Today that criticism has ceased.

Music that is often called intellectual, like that of Johann Sebastian Bach, for example, may also have a powerful emotional appeal. The sheer extent of variation and the intensity of emotion aroused by a certain kind of music do not seem to be diminished even if the music has a marked intellectual appeal. But perhaps music with an intellectual appeal is less erotic? The so-called intellectual qualities of music seem to be mainly connected with the structure of a composition, while the erotic ones are identified with the notes and characteristics of melody. The intellectual qualities of a performing artist can emerge through his ability to alternate between immediate feelings and "cold" judgment during his performance. The latter, among other things, might be expressed in an ability to interpret a composition for the piano in different ways.

To take an example that might illustrate this point: a text with strong emotional appeal for Peter and Paul can make them quite dogmatic about the possibilities of interpretation. Peter: "It is obvious that this is the only way that this can be interpreted." Paul: "No, no, no. It is quite clear that . . ." It is considered intellectual to be able to juggle with many possibilities, even if one is emotionally engaged. A not inconsiderable part of intellectual life consists of well-articulated verbal clashes between advocates of different interpretations, whether of words or of music.

I will never forget a tragic little incident that happened to me in the realm of music. It directly concerns the clash of interpretations. My music teacher had a pupil whom he had brought as far as that great event, the debut on the concert platform. Beforehand, I was allowed to listen to and comment on her interpretation of Beethoven's *Pathétique* Sonata, op. 13. The company was pleasant and relaxed. But then something terrible happened. My dear teacher knew a music critic—but not well enough, as it turned out. The critic was invited to listen to the pupil play. He proved to be obsessed with a particular interpretation of the famous opening of the sonata. He absolutely rejected any hint of rallentando, that is to say, a little slower tempo at certain points. On that account he started a metronome. But with the best will in the world, the pianist could not play according to the metronome, nor did it suit her particular personal interpretation. She was on the verge of tears, and it was only a fortnight before her debut. Her nervousness was unbearable.

Her debut was so-so. One of the worst things that can happen is to be exposed to cocksure, blinkered criticism just before a vital performance. In this case, both the debutante and the critic were emotionally trapped by their professionally defensible interpretations, but the latter behaved in an arrogant and unfeeling manner. This little story is meant only as an introduction to a defense of amateurs' complete liberty to let emotions dominate their interpretations. The fact is that music offers endless possibilities for finding one's own path in and about the world of sound. I would suggest only one limitation: one ought to show consideration for family and neighbors.

It is sometimes astonishing how little faith one might have in one's own emotions and how ruthlessly they can be put aside. An amateur forces himself to play a piece faster than is technically required. He reads the instruction "allegro molto," or something else menacing, and races off. It is easy to hear that the performance seems hurried and unfeeling. But in essence what does speed mean? What the composer or publisher has written about tempo and the like ought to be irrelevant to the amateur. Try andante if allegro molto is impossible. If you want to play Chopin's *Revolutionary* Etude, you can choose a relatively slow tempo and change it where it feels best *for you.* You are not giving a concert. In any case, you will preserve the structure.

It is obvious that that which is created by a great composer, or expresses a particular style, encompasses a musical world that is big enough for many of us. But respect can easily become a hindrance. For example: obviously I admire the giants in the history of philosophy, but I don't submit to them. Their thoughts are the stuff of genius, no doubt, but the material has to go through my poor brain. If heart and mind are in doubt and say "perhaps," I will adopt only what I myself consider really true and appropriate. I regard music in the same way.

It is said of many people that they live by music and that music is their life. That seems to imply that for them a day without music is not a good day. The social and religious significance of music all year round is most striking in societies ruled by traditions. African cultures have become better known and respected through the central role played in them by music and dance. The student uprising in Berkeley, California, in 1968 was characterized, among other things, by the sound of music everywhere. In the buildings and the streets, even on the roofs, round the clock. I know that, because I was a visiting professor there in that particular year.

Just in this century, speculations about the meaning of words and sentences have inspired thousands of books and articles in the field of the philosophy of language. The inner meaning of music has given rise to far fewer theoretical analyses. But because music can be said to be full of meaning, it is an obvious philosophical task to describe this type of meaning and its relation to other types.

Between the ages of four and eight, I liked to sit under the family's big Steinway grand piano and to listen to my dear brother play. He was eleven years older. The first movement of Beethoven's so-called *Moonlight* Sonata made a strange and deep impression. The experience was the origin of a point of view that I firmly espoused in later years: that music expresses thoughts fully and directly, whereas language has to make a detour via words. Music says something straight out! Is it misleading to say so? After all, music uses notes to express meaning. Is this not a regrettable devaluation of language? Of course. I looked down on language. School assignments in essay writing and Norwegian literature were intended to train the ability to express oneself and appreciate belles lettres and poetry. But I thought that what we were being trained to do was miserable compared with the expressive power of music.

Within me formed the conviction that in a piece of music at the level on which I was concentrating, there was an almost limitless potential. Consequently I believed that it would suffice to stick to a few of the great composers and a few of the great compositions. This attitude had a ridiculous outcome when I sought admission to the famous academy of music in Vienna. Besides mountain climbing, I proposed cultivating music in Austria. I played two pieces at the entrance audition, one of which was Rachmaninov's C Minor Prelude. For many years I had listened to and practiced the two or three pieces that I now played. After the audition I was placed in a master class, where there were only three others—and they were professionals. I had not the slightest chance in that company, but a professor had arranged the impossible.

For six weeks things went well, because I chose to play pieces that I pretended not to have played before. After a week I deliberately played the first piece badly, and after two or three weeks, as well as I could. The professor, a somewhat excitable man, did not grasp that I was cheating. But I had hardly any repertoire, so after six weeks I wrote that I had to go back to Norway because my grandmother was dead. I could not bring myself to write "Meine Mutter ist tod," which would have made my departure rather more understanding and convincing.

The Role and Status of Values in Life

In ethics we distinguish between value objectivism (or realism) and value subjectivism (or emotionalism). The latter implies that the declaration of value is merely an expression of the preferences of particular people or groups. In short, objectivism is based on the proposition that there are true values independent of differing opinions of their nature.

Reality can be considered as socially constructed reality or as a reality that exists independently of all social conditions. Without using elevated language, we may perhaps say that some of us have a tendency to add, in all modesty, "In my view . . ." or "I feel that . . ." when we talk, while others say, "It's like this" or "This is the case." Value objectivism maintains that there are values in the same way as there are numbers, not only figures, and that ideas exist in the way Plato seems to have conceived them. In postmodernism on the other hand, the social relativism of ethics seems to have been accepted. Values are social in character. Philosophical postmodernists, however, must probably concede that the concept of social construction is itself a social construction.

A scale of values must be colored by feelings in order to function at all. In a somewhat critical situation in a small boat at sea, a friend suddenly said to me, "I don't want to die here!!" The manner in which these words were uttered revealed intense emotion, hence the two exclamation marks. The remark was perhaps above all the prelude to an outburst of opinion and a proposal for action: "We must turn back!" Because he wanted us to turn back. The power lay in the intensity of will more than in that of emotion. The declaration was the reverse of a playful remark. All joking aside—we must turn back! It is impossible to avoid smiling at the thought of the remark about dying, but it was a serious comment in a critical situation. And we turned back.

In our history books we learn that the Enlightenment put reason on a pedestal and optimistically believed that it could ensure progress on all fronts, even where values were concerned. This point of view has subsequently been ridiculed and declared naive. As far as I can make out, a return to such times is desirable, but obviously only if we mean a reason and a critical faculty that are based on deeper, value-oriented premises. In that case, emotions are involved with power, since a value-oriented life is an emotion-oriented life. We are fond of our values and experience a kind of creative pleasure when we manage to realize them. Without a constant appeal to reason, this is impossible, allowing for a sense of discernment—a critical and constructive attitude with a good dose of self-criticism. In a friendly atmosphere, you can stand a great deal from other people.

As human beings we have values and a scale of values. The mere fact of having them is characterized by positive feelings. And we are worried at the thought of losing a sense of values. Values or a sense of values can be lost and regained, individually and socially. We realize our values as well as we can, or we dislike neglecting them. Our values alter with age. This alteration is wholly or partly conscious. If some of childhood's values persist in later years, we admit it, with a smile perhaps—or stoutly deny it.

This is a suitable point for a digression on preserving a child's values. In a teenage group to which I belonged, we looked down on adults with some contempt. We used the expression "the grown-ups" with a smile, and somewhat arrogantly as a term of opprobrium, that is to say, a word for something with a negative emotional tone. We were truly overcome with revulsion at the prospect of becoming grown-up. Perhaps that contributed to the fact that in so-called adult years, with mounting seriousness and energy, I persisted with habits and opinions of a childlike, or rather childish and ludicrous, kind. This had social consequences, since the world expected that, as a professor, I would display professorial behavior. Luckily I did not have a taste for behaving myself in a manner that could be interpreted as unbecoming when I lectured. My motto was "Look professorial and therefore appear with collar and tie." Occasionally, if I forgot my tie, I borrowed one from a student. Nobody was to be seriously offended by deviation from the norm.

But it is difficult to avoid offending someone. Not too late in life, I realized that many people who appear to be socially successful often have a surprisingly limited self-esteem. "Thin-skinned" is a not entirely appropriate epithet, but one is tempted to use it in this case.

Against this I advance the following proposition: compared with what might be called an average living creature, like a worm or a fly, each one of us has the mental equipment and genius very close to the level of a Leonardo da Vinci or an Albert Einstein. And it has taken hundreds and hundreds of millions of years to create something as talented and with such unbelievably great potential as a human being.

A Conflict between Emotions and Logic?

By considering the limitations in the way we justify our view of life, we can take a step further in our consideration of the relation between feeling and cognition. Every living creature has its own intrinsic value is an axiom of mine. I should say that this expresses an intuition. On the other hand, I am perfectly well aware that not everybody accepts it. Some people do agree, while saying that it is only a feeling that they have. Here I take the middle ground. It is misleading to say "only." An intrinsic value is *obvious* to me, in the sense that it provides a clear justification for me to do something for the living creature's own sake, and that alone. I believe that I perceive the intrinsic value. But I call it an axiom because I cannot find a proof. It is nothing more or less than an intuition. When people say that one must justify one's fundamental principles, it is well to be able to quote Aristotle's statement that it shows a lack of upbringing to believe that one can justify everything.

It is usual to quote examples of how emotions lead to rejection of all logic, how those who are driven by their emotions are forced to abandon all logical principles. I am often forced to admit that the examples are appropriate, but not under the circumstances in which they are applied. Luckily, emotions and logic can work well together, but both can also be equally misleading. Let us take an example. Supposing we are standing at a crossroad, discussing whether such-and-such a place lies to right or left. First we try turning left, but it does not lead us to our destination. Consequently the right-hand path must be the correct one. The logical structure is this: "Either A or B. Not A, hence B." Such a proposition may easily appear convincing. A feeling of incontrovertibility can emerge and overwhelm us in the same way as emotions do. This particular example has a simple structure. But it is more important to see how a slightly more complex logical structure can mislead. That is to say, it will convince us about something for which neither logic nor anything else will provide a justification for being convinced. In the simple example I mentioned, we ignore the possibility that neither path will lead to our goal. The protagonists have simply not felt that a third possibility can exist.

A similar situation arises when we say that a feeling dominates a decision. In a certain sense we may also say that we are misled by our feelings. But in addition we could justifiably say that it is not the feeling itself that is misleading, in the same way that in the above-mentioned example the fault does not lie in the logic itself. At the crossroad one person says, "To the left! To the left!" He is overcome by the memory of a charming view along the way. The others let themselves be influenced by him, and they all go off happily to the left. Exactly as in logic, there is nothing intrinsically wrong with the feeling. It is our attitude to the feeling that is somewhat faulty. All honor to the memory of a lovely view.

I would however venture to advance a general proposition: in our type of intelligence-dominated culture, it is easier to be misled by logic than by emotions. A fundamental reason for that which is seen as a conflict between feeling and logic is that we do not take the time to articulate with reasonable clarity what we believe. From a philosophical point of view, a number of situations that we face in life are so complicated and varied that very few people are in a position to develop prescriptive systems that, to a certain degree, offer precise guidance in concrete circumstances. Here the medieval philosopher Thomas Aquinas is the great master. From my point of view, philosophical texts can give inspiration today in many different contexts, but it is unrealistic to expect comprehensive guidance. Thomas Aquinas could assume that everyone was Catholic, but we cannot do so. And the conditions of society change with a speed that makes it difficult to stick to particular concrete guidance in the manifold variety of the types of situations in the tapestry of life.

A human life and we ourselves are like a *current* rather than something rock solid. With comparatively reasonable justification we may say that in particular circumstances we wish to be rock solid. But in a number of other circumstances, we may say that we do *not* try to be like a rock but rather to be pliable. When I look back, I admire the Norwegian King Haakon's firm rejection of any compromise with the Nazi occupation authorities during the German invasion from April to June 1940. In the fight for what we believe is right and proper, we must absolutely be rock solid. At the same time, we must always be open to the possibility that we have made a mistake, and be adaptable when new, relevant circumstances arise. They do so absolutely all the time. Thus only *an open mind* will suffice.

Feelings That Create the Drive to Research

Scientists and scholars can say something like, "You feel that such-and-such is true, but research indicates that you are wrong." Like others they can be arrogant, but they can also show understanding and say, for example, "More research is needed in this field," or "Well, yes, I believe there is something in what you feel, and further research might confirm it." They might even go so far as to say, "I admire you for having your own opinions in this matter, defying science." I approve of an organization like Alternative Network. They publish works with really imaginative assumptions without paying particular regard to what most scientists think of the subjects in question—flying saucers, for example.

Perhaps we do not think often enough about the connection between the fervor of the specialists and their emotional commitment and maturity. When the subject is psychology, the history of art, or some other field in the humanities, the emotional undercurrent is easier to understand than in the so-called exact sciences. If a mathematician reads about a solution in a professional journal, his appreciation of the method can release intense feelings. "The method is quite brilliant; I *must* try to do something similar." If the inspired mathematician himself discovers a proof that is even more elegant, beautiful, or rigorous, feelings may well be at boiling point. But the conventions of present-day research preclude the publication of outbursts of emotion. It is not as it was during the Renaissance, when leading mathematicians were guilty of some cheating and nonsense, and were perfectly capable of admitting to emotions in print and on public occasions. They allowed emotions freedom of expression, especially in learned pamphlets. Viggo Brun's book *Everything Is Numbers* (published in 1964) quotes one of Lodovico Ferrari's pamphlets against Niccolò Fontana Tartaglia, both of whom were world-famous mathematicians. Ferrari wrote: "I believe that my last pamphlet has broken your backbone so thoroughly that you can just about twitch your tail. If you still have some energy left, it is time to show it, because otherwise you will spend the rest of your life sunk in a mire of dishonor, which will be celebrated as a triumph for ignorance and crime."

On the other hand, for a long time a clearly expressed gratitude to God was a constant ingredient in strictly scientific literature. Now the style of periodical literature has become more or less completely arid. We never find sentences like "And now I am going to draw a conclusion that will make you jump up and down with admiration," even if that is exactly what the author is hoping for. The conclusion is that of course professional mathematics can be marked by strong emotional undertones. If the emotional undertones more or less disappeared from the sciences, creativity and the speed of advance in those same sciences would be greatly reduced. But if one hesitates to call all our mathematicians emotional people, there is good reason.

The so-called "Aha!" experiences may be well concealed. This does not exactly lead to running out into the street shouting or cheering, or the equivalent in published papers.

So nowadays, as in the past, research can be driven by strong emotions. But one must not confuse the issues. If one is aiming for a doctoral degree in literature or philosophy, one need not dampen one's feelings; one can freely give expression to what one is really feeling. But expressions of admiration, contempt, respect, revulsion, and the like obviously cannot be advanced as arguments for or against a point of view. Few people have analyzed the distinction between an emotion and an argument so happily as the Norwegian existentialist philosopher Peter Wessel Zapffe (1899–1990). As a practicing lawyer in the 1920s, Zapffe learned to argue clearly from existing laws. He functioned *de lege lata,* that is, from given laws, not *de lege ferenda,* as lawgiver. Zapffe had to try to work out how an abstract and general legal formulation could be used, for example, in a concrete sentence in a particular case. This seemed a ridiculous and emotionally absurd occupation for an existentialist philosopher.

So he had to flee, and turn to something completely different. He began to write the work called *On the Tragic.* In its first version, as Zapffe himself said, the book was "simply the enunciation of a view of life," characterized by violent outbursts of emotion in the middle of cold argumentation. It was permeated with a positive attitude and, to an even greater degree, distinguished by emotionally charged sentences. In a later book, with the ironical title *How I Became So Clever and Other Texts,* from 1986, Zapffe wrote: "Everywhere personal conviction was a sufficient test of truth. This crusading atmosphere, which dominated the style of the manuscript [of *On the Tragic*], gradually had to give way to newer considerations." It was then that the distinction between emotion and argument was first introduced.

Zapffe wanted to carry out research and perhaps take his doctoral degree. He believed that I was useful in the reworking of the manuscript about the tragic. In *How I Became So Clever* he says, "The high school pupil and later graduate student Arne Naess proved to have opinions that were highly relevant to the new enterprise." Zapffe did not really know me as a high school pupil, but we found each other while rock climbing at Kolsås, outside Oslo, and combined forces in changing the form of his manuscript. However, we preserved the whole gamut of literary metaphors—and the powerful emotional charge of the work. Zapffe calls an uncritical mixing of emotionally charged proclamation and research "hybrid brain embryos." According to him, the two activities may well be combined: "On that account, it is consequently unnecessary to restrain any of one's vital impulses—it is only necessary to hoist the ensign that identifies the voyage." Vital impulses may result in emotional outbursts and simple assertion. Such things have their place in a thesis, not as arguments but as what they are: spontaneous value judgments. They must simply not pretend to be anything else.

Research: An Ocean of Unsolved Problems

What then about imagination, curiosity, and wonder in science, scholarship, and research? Given the way we feel about ourselves and the world, there is much with which we are discontented. But imagination, curiosity, and wonder are feelings that point in the opposite direction: they are states of affairs marked by positive feelings, where we give imagination free rein. In varying degrees, depending on the type of person we are, we all live by imagination, while at the same time, with greater or lesser ability, we cope with the small, practical realities of existence.

Research may be considered an extension and deepening of curiosity and wonder through the use of imagination. More science, more wonder. Isaac Newton put it this way: the scientist is like a boy playing on the seashore while the great ocean of truth lies undiscovered before him. Unfortunately curiosity, wonder, and imagination may take an immature direction. Children may pull off the legs of a fly one by one, or otherwise mishandle or kill animals out of curiosity. Adults can cause animals pain in the interests of research. And it is quite easy for very young people to become hardened, so that they gradually overcome an innate dislike of hurting animals or even human beings. In Nazi concentration camps during the Second World War, it was much easier to recruit very young people as guards and make them act brutally than to do the same with those older than thirty. The ethics of research aim at fixing limits to the systematized curiosity of modern science.

Those comparatively few people who have the opportunity to write poetry or carry out research can obtain good practical guidance in cultivating curiosity and continue with their work. In the philosophy of science we talk about theoretical imagination and constantly repeat that theories have a vital ingredient of imaginative quality. In other words, it is no use basing a theory exclusively on observations, irrespective of how many may have been made. Between the ages of six and twenty, young people are subject to pressure in the direction of being sober, down-to-earth, and practical in the narrowest sense. At school the succession and nature of historical events, insofar as we *know* why they happened, are presented as if they were facts, and predetermined into the bargain. In Norwegian schools, for example, there is still a lack of practice in developing the imagination. "What would have happened if Napoleon had won the Battle at Waterloo?" "What if America was 'discovered' three hundred or five hundred years later?" "What if Hitler had won?" One does not learn to ask such good questions. One does not learn to write about such good subjects today. But perhaps the situation will change?

Why do I bring imagination into the picture? Because taming imagination reduces the creative power of humankind. As a little instance of how we can and ought to regard the imagination of other people, consider the case of a physiotherapist of my acquaintance.

She encouraged her patient's ridiculous, unrealistic illusions, provided they were harmless. For example, she thought it was amusing and therapeutically fortunate that a certain male patient was obsessed by the thought of what handsome legs he had. This had favorably affected the way in which he did his exercises during the therapy sessions. And many exercises could be devised to focus on his legs. For her part, the physiotherapist could not see anything special in his legs but clearly acknowledged that his opinion intensified rather than reduced his innocent fantasies. It is often pedagogically useful to say, "Pretend that you are . . ." Emotions swing into action, and in many cases we can attain a three-stage process: imagination–positive feeling–learning.

Cultures that are essentially different from that in which the reader lives do not seem to make a clear distinction between what they call facts and what they allow to be imagination. I was once on an expedition whose purpose was to keep intact as a shrine the holy mountain Tseringma in Garwal Himalaya. We were suddenly joined by a couple of cheerful young local girls who wanted to follow us to a camp above their home. They walked barefoot through the snow. A native with a talent for languages allowed us to question them closely about whether they believed in the Abominable Snowman, who is said to wander among the mountains in that region. Was he fact or myth? It was impossible to get a straight answer. Some of their cheerfulness was due perhaps to the fact that such a form of questioning flouted good manners in their culture. But it was impossible for me to give up the thought that in parts of their mental world, a concept could be simultaneously *both* fact and myth. It was obvious that such a view of facts versus myths might stimulate imagination. It seemed to me that everyone we met in the little community helped in this way to add to the traditional way in which they experienced the world. The holy mountain was *both* a queen and a mass of minerals.

Merely to sense what something is, to stimulate the imagination about what the cosmos is according to present-day physics, can be culturally worthwhile. This is wholly consistent with the feeling that many physicists have that we don't really know what we're talking about. Those with a weakness for profound wonder have infinitely much to wonder about. The way our society is today, there is much talk about how difficult things are and how much knowledge and intelligence is needed to master urban life. Perhaps we ought also to consider how much discipline is required not to let imagination spoil time that has to be consecrated to serious work.

4 *Reason and Feeling Are Interactive*

> *Spinoza has a view of reason* (ratio) *that does not place it in contradistinction to the emotions. He distinguishes between "active" and "passive" emotions, corresponding roughly to what we call "positive" and "negative" emotions respectively.* Ratio *supports the active emotions and is indispensable for our quest for liberty. Spinoza is one of the thinkers in the history of the West who have been most concerned with the role of the emotions. In his view passive feelings do not engage the whole person—only the active ones do so. He believes that we can transform passive feelings into active ones.*

My attitude to Spinoza resembles that which I have toward Gandhi—taking account of both his writings and his life. The stories about Spinoza are just as uplifting in regard to his character as the tales of Gandhi's life. Both inspire confidence because, in part, not only did they produce words, but they acted out their philosophy of life.

My aim is to demonstrate how Spinoza's view of things may offer some fundamental pointers in constructing a philosophy of life adapted to our own age. I do not look upon his *Ethics* as a "gospel" of mankind and the world, but rather as a source of inspiration. I find much with which I do not disagree, but a number of thoughts appear alien and irrelevant. I do not wish to pretend that I fully understand the mental processes of a thinker from the seventeenth century, living in a completely different culture.

Baruch de Spinoza (1632–77) is *the* central figure in the history of Western philosophy where the emotions are concerned. It is he who has given them the greatest prominence in his writings. This applies particularly to the process that occurs when powerful feelings are involved in deciding a choice of action.

Spinoza is probably the least original of the great philosophers, but nonetheless everything he wrote has an original touch. Harry Austryn Wolfson, professor of philosophy at Harvard, set himself the task of investigating where Spinoza found his inspiration and ideas. He analyzed *Ethics* line by line and uncovered the sources of just about everything that Spinoza says. But he also showed that Spinoza modified everything that inspired him. There is much from oriental sources—names like Ibor Ezra, Ibor Gabriol, Leo Hebraeus, Maimonides, Shakrastari. Spinoza's Jewish parents came to Holland from Portugal, so there was a strong Arabic influence on his upbringing. Where Western models are concerned, he was influenced by medieval philosophy. A careful study of his Latin requires insight into medieval Latin. For instance, a verb like *naturare,* literally "to make natural," will hardly be found in the Latin of the ancient world.

Among other things, this book is inspired by Spinoza's firm belief in humanity's potential when we are acting strictly in accordance with what is imprinted in our nature and avoiding everything else. This attitude is in stark contrast to the skeptical, not to say pessimistic, view of a human being that is prevalent in a materially affluent country: to believe in real progress is usually dismissed as naive. It is generally accepted that we must overcome the belief of the Enlightenment in progress and reason, if we have not already done so. The very foundation of Spinoza's ethics is a belief in the possibility of the individual's making progress. Toward the end of his life, he was nonetheless worried by the power of politically authoritarian and dictatorial trends, and their potential effect on the individual human being. In his view, he was witnessing a societal change that was moving in a vicious circle. But there is no hint that his view of emotional life had altered. People who knew him seem to have credited him with a light temperament.

Without Feelings, No Change

Spinoza believed that human nature is such that the sight of others' happiness releases happiness in ourselves—and on the other hand the sight of sorrow releases sorrow. But at the same time a human being has unbounded ability to display envy, which is a "passive" emotion in relation to our nature because it does not develop any of our essence. In someone who is envious, for example, sorrow can be triggered by the sight of someone else being happy, while unhappiness may trigger pleasure. Such being the case, there is something wrong with that person's emotional life. Nonetheless, just as in the case of happiness, there are different forms of unhappiness. An ordinary feeling of sadness affects only parts of the soul, while melancholy, as Spinoza uses the word, touches the entire soul.

The word *passive* in the expression "passive emotion" may perhaps be provocative or confusing, because it may justifiably be maintained that there is activity to a high degree in emotional states like hatred and envy. But they are passive in the sense that they do not develop our essential nature. If the term *activeness* is applied to the process of developing our essential nature, then it may justifiably be said that there may be great activity *without* our being in a state of activeness. In organized excursions into the countryside, there is great emphasis on activities, but not on activeness. To do a great many things is not enough; what is important is what we do and how it happens. It is those of our actions which affect our whole nature that I call activeness.

According to Spinoza only the positive emotions are effective, because they directly activate a human being's essential nature. He says that we can be slaves of negative emotions *(passiones)*. We might, for example, be overwhelmed by ill will. We can try to break loose from it, but it is there nonetheless. "You might as well give up trying to change Peter where such-and-such is concerned. . . . He's quite hopeless." When a society is dominated by the negative emotions, there may be a tendency to choose leaders animated by hatred. This affects the population. To Spinoza emotions may be intense and lead to actions like the use of violence, for example. But irrespective of how much activity is caused by hatred, such a phenomenon cannot emerge from the whole man. It can never wholly possess us. In his *Ethics* Spinoza says, "No evil can befall a person except through external causes."

Spinoza classifies hope as a passive emotion—which may surprise some people. Perhaps his point lies in demanding a tougher line in the maturing of emotions—that we must do something, be active, in order to realize the unlikely, not put our faith in what is very likely vain hope. Those who habitually talk about their hopes are perhaps in reality not especially active at all. Really active people have little time to articulate hope. In my view, on the other hand, hope is a decidedly active emotion. When we strive for or attain a goal in tune with our nature, our relation to that goal is activated.

To Spinoza apathy is a form of spiritual death. Apathetic people are alive in a biological sense, but nothing vital can happen to them. To gain in freedom, or any other aspect of the human essence, is impossible. They simply keep themselves alive. Spinoza dared to construct his ethics in such a manner that the absence of emotion becomes a state in which we stagnate in our development as human beings. No images can quite cover the relation between thoughts and feelings, but Spinoza has a useful suggestion: the rider gives orders to his horse, but it is the horse that takes him where he wants to go. Thoughts are like the rider, emotions like the horse. We believe that thoughts spur us to do things, but according to Spinoza, together with other greater and lesser prophets, they must stimulate feelings if anything is to happen. Dynamism is also found in the word *emotion,* which is derived from the Latin verb *movere,* "to move."

Thus we have a hypothesis which may be expressed in a mere four words: "Without feelings, no change." The road to freedom requires motivation through feeling or, as we have repeatedly seen, what Spinoza calls the transformation *(transformatio)* of feelings. One listens to what reason and experience have to say. What is experienced when one follows the voice of *ratio* is that which accompanies one's essential nature, and new experience requires new decisions. We try to follow *ratio* in the new circumstances. If that succeeds, we acquire yet more experience. As a result, empirical investigation also finds a place in Spinoza's philosophy.

Transformation of a negative emotion to a positive one can have great consequences for the processes of maturing in emotional life. What then is the significance of negative feelings in the development of such a process? We must become better acquainted with the negative feelings, particularly the kind of circumstances in which they appear. Why do I feel exactly this way?

Many people will say that anger can be a good thing. "To see our finest places polluted or 'developed' makes you angry, and that anger is a good thing," says Michael Soulé, a pioneer in the expanding conservation biology movement in the United States. Had he not become angry, he would not have become an environmental activist. Others may feel horror on being faced with destruction. The emotion gives rise to a decision to act, to join a movement to stop that destruction

Usually, however, to act resolutely needs a state characterized by negative feelings. As Martin Luther once said, we cannot avoid evil thoughts, but we can prevent their building nests in our heads. Spinoza omits dealing with something that is often heard. To take an example: "It was lucky that I had that setback, with all the bad, negative feelings that followed. It forced me to change my life for the better." Or: "It was extremely painful, but it helped me to see that life is not only a bed of roses." Or again: "I needed that defeat to show me that I was on the wrong path. So I am glad that it happened."

A lot of us use negative emotions like unhappiness, *angst,* and depression in a constructive way. Not a few have stories to tell about what they have learned in a time of suffering. There are many who are even grateful for having seen the dark sides of life. Intrinsically, according to Spinoza, unhappiness is not desirable. In the right context—for example, when someone close dies—sorrow is not in opposition to human nature. It is vital, however, to work on sorrow—for example, by carrying out duties that demand, if not exactly good humor, at least the absence of complaints and irritation. In a word, the transition from and conversion of negative emotions to positive ones must not be accomplished so that the former are denied a complex function and recognized as indispensable within the framework of a dignified human life.

Children who are overprotected against pain and disappointment may have reason to regret it later in life. But that does not mean that we ought to throw children into painful or frustrating circumstances—even if in general it may have desirable consequences. In short, negative feelings do *not* have intrinsic worth. They may have a functional value as more or less intentional "hardening." But generally it is only when we look back that we can detect that positive value of such emotions.

According to Spinoza, awareness of the cruelty that takes place and the terrible decisions that are made must be accompanied by unhappiness and other negative emotions. But it is obvious that if one enters into an active relationship with what is terrible, so to that extent do the negative emotions vanish.

As I interpret Albert Camus's book *The Plague,* it offers a sophisticated solution to the problem of evil. The hero of *The Plague* is a doctor who quickly grasps the gravity of the situation and swings into action where he believes that he can achieve something. As an analogy, someone who is concerned about drug addiction, criminality, psychopathy, and destructive tendencies makes short work of it all and asks himself: Is there anything that I can do in one of these fields? Can I give it a higher priority than anything else? If the answer is yes, one becomes active in relation to a problem and gets pleasure out of it.

Thus Spinoza's teaching may come to roost, but I believe one of his weaknesses is that he does not deal more thoroughly with the theme of how forms of *tristitia*, passive emotions, may have so-called instrumental value, and lead to something else and be of use in the path to higher states of freedom.

The Active Emotions Expand Our Degree of Freedom

To Spinoza people are not born free. The road to freedom is long, requiring experience and training. Greater insight into one's own negative feelings and their destructive effect can lead to their replacement by positive feelings. The setbacks of the past *can* be of benefit. We understand that we have a self that is being developed. More freedom implies that, to a greater degree than before, we are the cause of our own decisions. External influences are under control. More and more, one acts on something that lies in one's own nature.

The existence of a sense of community, and hence a peaceful society, depends on the presence of positive emotions. It also requires the existence of free men, and the possibility of spreading freedom. The minds of our fellow human beings, according to Spinoza, "are conquered not with weapons but with love and generosity." A good society may be considered as something that arises when circles of friends are extended. Friends wish one another well, are pleased when others are happy, and are saddened by others' sorrow. In this way they are acting in harmony with the nature and essence of mankind. Happiness, more freedom, and deepened friendship go hand in hand. The active emotions promote the feelings of community, and hence what we call moral conduct, as a consequence of natural causes. When we have little freedom, and strongly developed passive emotions, a morality based on a sense of duty is more necessary, a morality where unquestioned duty plays a central role. Maintaining a sense of community requires more authority and respect for "the moral law." A variation of this may be expressed in this way: "The action which you decide under particular circumstances must be such that you want everyone else in exactly the same kind of circumstances to be able to act in the same way that you do." One must not demand special treatment for oneself!

In establishing personal goals, it is worth asking if there is anything common to humanity that may be quite simply defined. We are accustomed to hear about happiness and self-realization. In Spinoza we find eight concepts that express how the active emotions affect the vital goals and values that he defines. They follow here—and the order can easily be changed:

1. To be understood on the basis of what one is rather than by something else. One does not want what one does, what one has done, and what one decides to be interpreted on grounds of something external or something alien to oneself.
2. To be active rather than passive in relation to that which concerns oneself.
3. To be the cause of something rather than to be the effect of something. This is closely related to the previous guideline.
4. To have the ability to achieve what one tries to achieve—to have the power to do so. This is essentially the condition for the foregoing qualities.
5. To be free.
6. To carry out and finish off what one tries to achieve.
7. To do what one is entitled.
8. To uphold and maintain that which one wants to be.

Now we have reached a critical point in Spinoza's philosophy of emotion. If one is not in some kind of emotional state, that is to say, if one is apathetic or completely neutral, one is stagnating as a person.

Every single movement in the direction of the eight goals thereby disappears. If emotions are negative, there is a process that removes one of the concepts from the eight, and the stronger and more dominant the process, the more can be lost. With positive emotions, it is the other way about.

More freedom is an indispensable goal for human beings, and for Spinoza the concept of freedom has an internal relation to other concepts. The most important thing is *esse in se,* being in oneself. This is in contrast to being in something else, *esse in alio.* The commandment "Be thyself," as elaborated by Ibsen, is not unknown in Norway. When we talk about the path to freedom that goes via active emotions, it is also a path that expresses the seven other goals. Close to the being in the self there is the expression "to understand what you do on the basis of what you are." But one can attain a more profound understanding of oneself and achieve a more comprehensive understanding of something else starting from oneself.

Spinoza's God—and Three Forms of Understanding

With the aid of some "technical" concepts, I will now present my interpretation of Spinoza's concept of God. It diverges from the interpretation of most Spinoza specialists. I need this in order to cast more light on Spinoza's view of the relation between humans and Nature. In an extension of the concept of God, I will briefly touch on how Spinoza distinguishes between three forms of understanding. In this way, perhaps, it will be a little easier to perceive how he relates emotion and reason.

Spinoza's definition of *Deus,* God, can easily become abstract, because it embraces a great deal. It is easier to consider words that mean the equivalent of *Deus.* To take an example, Spinoza says that the fundamental proposition that God is the creative force of Nature corresponds to the saying, "Nature's creative force is God." Here we find one proposition worth particular attention: *Deus est natura nat-*

urans. The meaning is not difficult to grasp, but how do we translate it? The word *naturans* is simply the present participle of the profoundly telling verb *naturare*—"to make natural"—mentioned earlier. A definition of *Deus* might then read, "God is the creative force in Nature." To put it another way, *Deus,* as the word is used in Spinoza's main work, is an expression of that which is considered to be what is creative in a constantly changing Nature. By emphasizing such a formulation, we avoid the widely held belief that by *God,* Spinoza simply meant Nature, or that the true God is Nature as a whole. Those who interpret Spinoza in this way usually attach the term *pantheistic* to his view of *Deus;* that is, God is everything. But Spinoza himself refers with approval to the Christian thought that God is *in* everything, and that everything is *in* God. This makes Spinoza a panentheist (God is *in* everything). That is to say that there is something of God as the creative force in all living things.

One of my main points is that Spinoza's God is not a being who created the world at some time in the past, a being who is fundamentally anything else but natural. Spinoza's God is said to be "immanent," in or of Nature, and not "transcendental," beyond and above it. Creation is always in progress, and *God* is the word for everything that is creative. Humans are not outside God, but our essence and nature are true parts of God's essence and nature. We are participants in the creative process, a part of *natura naturans.* The world is being created here and now; all living things take part in it. There is little difficulty in seeing how a Spinozistic concept of God may be felt to raise the status of human beings. We are not only creatures (as *natura naturata,* using the perfect participle of *naturare*), but creators. The world is always in the making, and we can cheerfully take part in the work.

Since individual beings are the only expression of God in the finite world, love of God cannot manifest itself in any other way than in relation to these individual beings. Love of God is, as I have said, a genuine part of human essence and self-realization, at the same time that humankind's essence is a genuine part of the infinite God's essence. Therefore we can say that we are "finite gods" in a somewhat diluted sense. Our development, however, cannot be infinite. We do not become at one with God.

Living creatures other than human beings can also become more perfect and realize their nature as a part of God's being. Each goes his own way, *sva marga* in Sanskrit. The cat unfolds in a catlike way, the lion in a lion way, the caprifolium plant in a caprifolium-like way. Spinoza himself mentions the horse as an example. It has *its* way. It feels, but its emotions are so different from ours that a true friendship between it and us can never arise.

In an extension of the interpretation of Spinoza's concept of God and that concept's relation to humanity and Nature, I will briefly present Spinoza's three forms of understanding or "cognition." The first is the cognition that the senses give us. The second concentrates on common qualities in classes of things, and mistakes are possible. The third is intuitive and not open to error.

The second type corresponds with that which *we* call scientific cognition. The third has no exact equivalent today. Yet it is the highest form, and our mental "power" reaches its zenith in it. Spinoza's celebrated term for it is *amor intellectualis*. The thorough treatment of Spinoza's philosophy in this book is largely motivated by his introduction of the third way of understanding. The verb *intellegere* may best be translated "to understand," and the corresponding noun *intellectus*, "understanding." *Intellectualis* must not be translated "intellectual." That is an adjective often used today in opposition to understanding. This is what Spinoza calls intuitive understanding of the particular, and it is distinguished from the exact sciences, which are concerned with the general. *Amor intellectualis* does not imply a distinction between feeling and reason. In *amor intellectualis, amor* and *intellegere* melt into one single whole. As I interpret *amor intellectualis,* it is not a subspecies of *amor* but a unified emotional understanding—understanding and emotion in an internal relation.

In Spinoza a separation of cognition and emotions is admittedly present in the first and the second form of cognition, but not in the third and highest form. In what Spinoza calls understanding love, we understand something in God's perspective, based on the creative force in nature *(natura naturans)*. A strange thing about comprehending love is that somehow it derives from the thought of *Deus.* It includes something in the framework of the everlasting and creative.

Is Mankind Good by Nature?

To achieve a convergence of reason and feeling ought to be a goal in our kind of society, where intellectual development in its narrowest sense seems to have received far too great a role compared with emotional development. This is true not least in a human being's formative years, say between five and fifteen.

To some extent, perhaps the environmental movement can help to form concepts that fuse insight and emotion. If we say, "Hallingskarvet is a great mountain," deliberately using the word *great* instead of *big,* it implies a positive value judgment—and therefore a feeling of greatness. If we say "Hallingskarvet!" the intonation and so forth can make the word express enthusiasm or respect. But does the outburst also have insight? "The creative force in Nature" is an indication of something abstract in relation to the concrete Hallingskarvet. Anyhow, we focus on human nature, not Nature as interpreted in environmentalism.

The most important reason for bringing in Spinoza is his optimistic view of human nature. The development of the potential of our own nature has a positive emotional value. Consequently the active emotions have a flying start at birth. Restraining influences might be present, but in that case they come from outside. A fundamental objection to Spinoza is that humankind is *not* good by nature, but evil. Even quite young children may strike each other and take pleasure in someone else's pain. There are those who believe this must come from something deep in human nature. But external influence after birth is clear. Let us imagine that a father says to his little son, "You will soon have a little playmate." When the playmate eventually arrives, he turns out to be no playmate after all, but something useless. Worse still, the amount of loving care and attention the son receives appreciably diminishes. The new creature is clearly the cause. He is unquestionably a rival! The situation may trigger powerful negative emotions. The firstborn may actually revel in the other's crying. But understanding parents are acutely aware of the possibility of envy, counteracting it by manifest love. The fundamental objection to Spinoza is unsound.

Ratio: *The Voice of Our Own Nature and Essence*

It may be said that within us there is a kind of life-compass that helps us on the way to greater freedom. It not only shows us different directions, but points out the path along which we are to continue. What direction ought we to choose? This inner compass is what Spinoza calls *ratio.* This term may be translated as "the voice of reason," something that points in a direction that is consistent with the active emotions and in harmony with humankind's nature or essence.

As I understand the voice of *ratio,* it does not speak to us in words. On the other hand, we have a distinct *feeling* of what the right choice is to be. Since the choice involves an unfolding of our nature, that choice has a positive emotional tone. To Spinoza and many seventeenth-century thinkers, *ratio* therefore expresses something quite different from the present-day usage of *reason* in English—*Vernunft* in German, and the French *raison.* Among other things, it has something to do with intuition. *Ratio* does not argue for or against but points out the right choice. Instead of "point out," we can use Wittgenstein's concept of *zeigen,* "to show." *Ratio* shows us the direction taken by that decision which is in harmony with the nature of human beings and thereby with *natura naturans.*

In translating vital words created in a culture essentially different from our own, it is a common practice to use a particular word freely, hastening to explain that there is no exact equivalent in one's own language for what one is trying to translate. We can save the word *reason* from its contemporary straitjacket of petty, utilitarian, and instrumental action—emphasizing that it is *ratio* at which we are aiming. Since *ratio* is connected with emotions, especially love or *amor Dei,* it might probably help to raise the standing of emotions by comparison with our own miserable concept of reason.

Among other thinkers who espouse a similar usage of the word *ratio,* I would like to mention Jean-Jacques Rousseau (1712–78). Rousseau summarizes a tragic event in his childhood roughly in this way: "Imagine a child, normally shy and obedient but dangerously proud and unpredictable in his passion—a child who had always been a child of the voice of reason." Rousseau seems to accept that it is consistent with the rules of reason to have intense and unpredictable emotions.

After the Industrial Revolution the voice of *ratio* continued to be heard and followed by a few influential philosophers. Subsequently this free voice of reason was reduced to deal with narrower and narrower concepts. It displayed an overpowering tendency toward a reduction to the voice of fluff rationality, rationality for trivial things. One example is the change in political economy from being an important branch of philosophy concentrating on economics to a severely quantitative science. Political economists are reluctant to venture onto thin ice and advance together with politicians. Among other things, this has been demonstrated in the debates on how to solve the environmental crisis.

The fundamental question is, What kind of reason and what kind of rationality do we really mean? From Isaac Newton's age onward, rationality has been closely associated with science and logic, not with thinking about values as a route to more fervent love of God. Today we think about rationality on the lines of the previously mentioned example of the rationality of building a parking lot. The chain of whys and wherefores is ignored. Rationality is instrumental and interpreted in relation to technical considerations, within a strict economic framework. If one questions the goals as defined, they turn out to be short-term, not related to ultimate values.

In other words, we must go deeper in examining the goals of pure rationality. One point is worth repeating: something is not rational unless it corresponds with the fundamental values and aims of our lives. That would mean a desirable step in the direction of accepting the principle that no policy is rational if it is not rational in relation to the most profound premises on which society is built. In other words, I assume that the statement "x is rational" is a type of relation within a normative system. A normative system is a synoptic presentation of the relation among our principles, our priorities, and the consequences of a decision. Only if a principle stands up to the test of these fundamental considerations will it be rational.

Those who espouse a particular action or a political program ought to do so on the assumption that what they are working for has a positive relation to our goals at the deepest level.

In a political debate there may be obvious dissension, but oddly enough, disagreement over the nature of the fundamental aims is rare. Consequently, we do not often discuss the most fundamental values of life and society. As a rule the most passionate conflicts originate at far more superficial levels. That does not affect the importance of probing deeply. There is much discussion about what forms of energy we ought to adopt if consumption continues to increase towards the year 2030, but we rarely ask if we ought not instead to concentrate on reducing the use of energy by each individual member of society. Here we are faced with ethical problems: consumerism and waste.

How then do we begin to follow the guidance for our actions which is contained in our innermost nature? That is what Spinoza asks us to do. We must listen to this voice of what he calls *ratio*. Without any effort on our part, there is something that, in particular situations, tells us which line of action conforms to our essential nature and which does not. It is a voice that resembles what we call the voice of conscience, the voice that warns, encourages, and instructs. If we are guided in this way, we act generously and grandly. To call Spinoza's viewpoint "rationalism" would be misleading today, because we associate being rational with denying the significance of emotions.

Contempt for Actions and Contempt for Human Beings

If, like Spinoza, we consistently believe that human nature is basically the same for everyone, it means that we can see a potential friend in every single person, as Gandhi did. In Norway during the Second World War, some members of the resistance movement once captured two Norwegians who were collaborating with the Nazi occupation authorities. The collaborators had served as torturers, or at least had mishandled some patriots. They explained how miserable they were now because of the deeds of which they had been guilty. I had the task of cross-examining them. At the end of the interrogation, one of them said: "Please help me, Professor Naess, and have me shot immediately!" This human being, a twenty-one-year-old Norwegian, went over to the German side when he was sixteen, through immature opposition to the majority of his fellow citizens. It is far from certain that he would have shown aggressive tendencies in other circumstances.

The best side of human nature is present even in "a bad lot," and that ensures the possibility of activating the positive emotions. After all, many saints displayed unfortunate tendencies when they were young. Their lives could have continued to be stamped by this if they had not undergone, more or less by chance, what may be called deep religious experiences of a rare kind.

From a Spinozistic point of view, a profound contempt for certain *actions* is something different from contempt for the *people* who perform them. Since two completely different things are involved, the word *contempt* ought to be used for one thing or the other in particular cases. The negative feeling applies to human beings or living creatures in general, while the negative judgment of an action depends on its conceptual classification. A transformation of emotions removes the one but naturally not the other. The matter is particularly obvious to those dealing with horrible crimes. In the function of a social worker, a clergyman, or a prison warden is such that it is impossible to maintain an ethically defensible level in contact with a criminal without changing a spontaneous feeling of contempt for a person to a feeling of horror at his terrible deeds, and a need to understand the development of his emotional life. Contempt for the person would adversely affect the work one has to do, in addition to which it would have a bad effect on one's own degree of freedom.

It is also central to Gandhi's view of emotions to distinguish between negative feelings for humans or other living creatures on the one hand and those same feelings toward their behavior on the other. He seems to think that a person as a whole is always more complete than the chance collection of deeds he has had time to perform. We do not have the time or opportunity to completely develop everything that lies within us, sometimes well hidden. Whatever we think of this, based on the views of both Spinoza and Gandhi, we can accept this fundamental principle: try to change your negative feelings toward a person to positive ones—appeal to what is good in your opponent's human qualities.

What is the reward of those who in a particular situation manage a transition from negative to positive feelings? A feeling of joy, for example. Joy is so intimately bound up with every transition from a negative to a positive emotional note that Spinoza has found it possible to propound the following definition-like saying: "Joy *(laetitia)* is the transition from a lower to a higher degree of perfection *(perfectio)*." But the strength of this feeling is variable. The greater the active feeling, the greater the increase of freedom, power, and understanding.

5　A Feeling for All Living Beings

It is not only our attitude to other human beings that
reveals our deepest values and highest priorities. It is also
our relation to all other living things. I believe that which
unites all forms of life is more important than that which
divides. I will try to illustrate how feelings for places and
feelings for other creatures can develop us as people. We can
learn to regard ourselves as something more than merely
ego. Better still, few are able to stay aloof and wholly
disregard the social self.

During a climb on a difficult section of a mountain, two friends
enter into a discussion of the aims and means of the enterprise. Bad
weather seems to be threatening. One wants to turn back, the other
to continue.

> *Peter:* I feel that it is the right thing to turn back. I feel that something
>   is not quite right here.
> *Elsa:* What on earth makes you feel that way? I don't feel like that.
>   And the aim of our expedition is the same as before. It can be a
>   great experience for us to reach the summit together.
> *Peter:* Well, you see, our aim is to get to the top, but *only* under
>   acceptable circumstances.
> *Elsa:* We have told our sponsors that our aim is to reach the top.
> *Peter:* It is also a defeat to continue in an irresponsible way. Something

in me says that it would not be sensible to carry on. We're approaching the limit of what is sensible. It's irrational to continue!

Elsa: But I seem to remember that you said that you felt that something was not quite right. What has that got to do with being sensible? You heard the weather report, and the prospects seem good. And with all our equipment, I can't see that it isn't sensible to carry on.

Peter: I agree that it would be sensible to carry on, on the basis of what you say. But where the mountain is concerned, my inner voice says something different. The weather is not bad, but the wind has veered, and it promises to continue doing so in an ominous direction—there's going to be a storm. If the mist keeps rising up the valley, we will have snow. Yes, the weather is good now, but I have a feeling that we will risk our lives on the descent even if we reach the top.

Elsa: But isn't your feeling subjective, and aren't you projecting it into the situation? It's not at all certain that it is the objective truth. I feel something completely different.

Peter: No, finding the objective truth is not the point. You yourself mention a feeling that you have. What are you basing *your* feelings on?

Elsa: I base them on our preparations, and the good weather that we actually have now, not on speculation about what horrible weather we might have later.

Peter: You may be right. In fact there is something within me that also wants to carry on, but I am going to turn back. *That* feeling is strongest. And in my book, to turn back doesn't mean the same as going back to the beginning of the expedition. We have been together with this mountain day and night. Aim and object are not the same. The object lies in the experience as a whole. Even if our sponsors believe that we ought to have carried on, it would not alter the fact that we made a responsible decision. It is not certain that reaching the physical summit of the mountain is "the top" in relation to my object in going on this expedition. But I believe it's sensible to go down.

Elsa: But I have decided to go on. See you in the camp.

Peter: See you then. Good-bye.

So one of them continued on for some time, while the other went down. In the event, the weather held for another day, and she who went on took some fantastic pictures. He who turned back discovered a rare insect that until then had never been found at such a great altitude.

This incident is a reminder that in a conflict, saying "I feel that . . ." is relevant and not irrational, and subsequent events may show that action based on that feeling may lead to a beneficial outcome. Reports on how and why accidents occurred on expeditions suggest that arguments of the kind characterized by "I feel that . . . ," uttered by those with long and varied experience, ought to be taken seriously.

Life as an Expedition

Life is such that again and again one has to find one's bearings and make important decisions on uncertain foundations. We do not have mastery over the future. It may not at all resemble the past. And the laws of nature are based exclusively on what has happened in the past and what is happening in the present. Differences of opinion are rarely settled on the basis of what we might consider as pure facts. Nor can we always hammer out precise hypotheses. One argument in a debate seems only a little more convincing than another. It *sounds* right.

The fact that a decision is based on intuition does not necessarily mean that it is suspect. On the contrary, decisions overflowing with arguments may be inferior, because, among other things, the circumstances are so complicated that we cannot manage to describe them properly with the help of words. Even if we characterize a decision as sensible or wise, it is not often that we can say that a few definite, weighty arguments have decided the matter. To take an example: A friend of yours wants to get married, and asks for advice. Ought he to do so? After much cogitation, for and against, perhaps you will say, "When all is said and done, I have a feeling that you ought to do so."

Some of us think that going through life is like meeting a succession of challenges, rather like being on an expedition—let us say an attempt to reach the top of an extremely high, unclimbed mountain. It assumes the keenest pleasure at the thought of reaching the summit, pleasant daydreams about the landscape, the view, a feeling of pride, or at least self-respect on reaching the top, and much else. In this case the summit can be conceived as either the physical summit or merely being on the mountain. Some of the challenge of such an expedition lies in carrying it out without the risk of serious injury to body and soul. The value of complete physical and mental well-being must obviously be given a higher priority than that of attaining the expedition's intended goal. The pleasure of mastering the challenges under way must be balanced against the suffering and disappointment when something goes wrong. For something usually does go wrong. At the start of an expedition, there is often a fixed plan with aims and objects, something predetermined. This holds even if the expedition is purely a reconnaissance. In conformity with the possibilistic attitude to life—everything is possible, anything can happen—we can say that life emerges as we live it. To the questions "Who am I?" "What am I?" "What do I want to be?" it may perhaps seem a bit odd to add "at the moment." But if one wants to characterize what happens in life as a *flow* of events, and for my part I think that it is fruitful, one must accept that there are strong elements of uncertainty and vacillation in any human life. A life seen as a rounded entity, especially in the comforting glow of hindsight, appears rather different from a life considered as a single expedition in a definite landscape.

It would be a peculiar expedition if the start were solely a matter of asking questions. At a complex railhead in north Pakistan, the members of the Norwegian Tirich Mir expedition in 1964 simply could not find the goods wagon with all their vital equipment. The questions rained down. What now? One of our more humorous members proposed that we each write a poem about an imaginary expedition and send them to our sponsors. They deserved something for their support. The idea gave us a good laugh. We clearly had the ability to see the situation from the point of view of a game. A game lost. But in the end we found the wagon and all the equipment. The completely open, indeterminate moment when we said to one another, "What on earth are we going to do—without equipment?" ended with a bang. Immediately we got going with the thousand and one different tasks that an expedition offers. Many similar situations appear in life when it is necessary to see different possible answers, but nonetheless we apply ourselves with nose to the grindstone when the decision is made.

Psychological vigor is absolutely critical for the mood of an expedition. It can switch from an intense positive feeling to the opposite. The expedition may seem to become meaningless, and in such a way that one regrets having come, in the same way as when one has to acknowledge a mistaken choice of career, study, or holiday destination.

Considered in its entirety, life can scarcely be seen as a single expedition, but rather it is a succession of different ones with varying aims and objects. But even that is simplifying in the extreme. Things have gone far indeed if one regrets that one has lived, even if, so to speak, it has been a matter of habit and without pleasure. In sober moments not a few will say something like: "Life? *Life?* Oh well, it goes on. I can't complain." Time passes. "What happened this year?

Last year? There was something after all." It is depressing to hear tired people talk about their tired lives. And they are well aware of this, so luckily they rarely complain to outsiders. Once, when I was going to speak at an old-age home, I was warned beforehand: "Don't talk about fatigue and illness. There is too much talk about it here." Encouragement, yes! No realism, thank you very much! We know that tens of thousands long to die. Some pray to God every night to be allowed to die, others beg for years for help to die, others again live on only from a sense of duty, yet others try in all earnest to end their lives of their own accord—not from a sudden attack of desperation, but after a long, carefully considered decision.

Back to the subject of expeditions. It is easy to overlook the emotional aspect of an expedition in favor of the results. Let us consider, for example, the expedition in 1995 to Drangnag-Ri, in the Himalayas, led by my nephew, Arne Naess "Jr." From a philosophical point of view, it was an unusually interesting expedition. Thanks to an openhearted book about it, the emotional aspect is laid bare. The expedition was intended as a tenth anniversary reunion of the members of the successful Norwegian Everest expedition of 1985. It soon became evident that strains that were felt as trivialities or merely amusing little hurdles in 1985 felt like huge and pointless exertions in 1995. The passage of ten years had changed the participants more than expected. The intense motivation, characterized by cheerfulness, what I call "the glow," had vanished. It is difficult to predict how differently you will react when you have become ten years older. The participants considered the changes to be somewhat ridiculous. Consequently, there was a good deal of smiling, laughter, and self-derisive remarks. Normally on an expedition, there are little daily incidents of good luck or the reverse, and unforeseen difficulties arise. On the whole, however, the "glow" surrounding the enterprise ensures that most things can be treated with good humor. One or two quotations illustrate the circumstances surrounding this "old boys' " expedition. I have found the extracts in Arne's book of the expedition, *Drangnag-Ri: The Holy Mountain.*

> Kjell Torgeir, Bjørn, Torger, and I are on our way from Advanced
> Base Camp to Camp 1. The glacier is like a microwave oven. The
> sun is burning, and the whole surface of the snow is reflecting every
> single ray. At an altitude of 5,700 meters, not much is filtered out. It
> is well nigh unbearable, I ought to have started earlier in the day.
>
> Why am I doing this? I am fifty-seven years old. What kind of
> a fool am I? This is a young man's game. Why am I not sailing, or
> playing golf or tennis? Why do I want to climb high mountains?
> I must love suffering. Besides which I must like having headaches,
> freezing at night and frying by day, and being exhausted and out
> of breath at the least exertion. Why am I here? Of course the view
> is fantastic, but hardly worth all the discomfort. I agree that it has
> a value of its own, but it is fairly academic. This is just another
> glacier, and not at all different from any other glacier, and it does
> not answer the question "Why?" Is it connected with the fact that
> I am a climber in heart and soul, and this is what climbers do?
> Between expeditions I forget all the misery and remember only the
> good times. Experiences that are even stronger than the external
> pain, and that are related to the companions who are with me. To be
> able to spend weeks together, doing what we all like, and are capable
> of doing, in surroundings we understand and take pleasure in, is
> something rather special. In my heart of hearts I know that if the
> others go to another mountain, I will join them regardless of the
> danger and discomfort. Our friendship began on a mountain, and it
> has a future among the mountains.

We may admit to being possessed of certain thoughts, certain actions, certain relations with other human beings. Under these conditions the consequences may be pain, sorrow, and despair, and are beyond our control. In the foregoing I have assumed that normally we aspire to happiness and want to avoid sorrow. But there is also something called being "possessed." In the book mentioned above, Arne Naess "Jr." expresses the state of being possessed in a certain way. But his life subsequent to writing it suggests that the sense of being possessed was not long lasting. The discomfort was too great. Age had changed him. It is not easy to foresee if and when a sense of being possessed will cease.

Does being possessed indicate that we are irrational by nature? No, but perhaps it shows that we can be slaves of negative emotions, as Spinoza puts it. I say "perhaps" because it is misleading to a certain degree to say that we are possessed by emotions. A person may periodically be possessed by the thought of death. Even if it is an extremely unpleasant state, it is somewhat misleading to say that it is a feeling by which a person is possessed. One is not possessed by a feeling, but by ideas, fantasies, and thoughts. On an expedition where everything seems to be going wrong, those manage best who remain active, but with calm in their innermost being. Such people manage to cope with an extremely difficult situation. They do not have intense feelings but a steady positive mood. I prefer to call it a "tone." Whatever the prevailing tension, there is always the positive tone on which to rely.

About expeditions to great mountain ranges like the Himalayas: I have been asked if something along the lines of the rules of mountain safety can be advanced as a kind of philosophy of life. In a not too serious mood, I established a set of rules for myself—closely related to the familiar wording of the rules of mountain safety:

1. Avoid enterprises that you are not mature enough to carry out within the framework of the values you are trying to uphold at all costs.
2. Whenever your actions or intentions affect both your own and others' interests, tell the others frankly.
3. Show respect and gratitude to those who try to give you good advice, even if you consider it to be bad.

4. Listen to those who already have experience of that kind of enterprise in which you are attempting to become involved.
5. Be well prepared for both success and different kinds of failure.
6. Try to articulate priorities. Foresee awkward dilemmas as well as you can.
7. Avoid becoming a lone wolf.
8. When you realize that you are on the wrong path, turn back. It is never a disgrace to turn.
9. Avoid overexertion. Find ways of reducing stress if it gets the upper hand.
10. The important thing is not adversity but how you cope with it.

As an admirer of deep cultural differences, and a rich variety of sustainable ways of living within a culture, I feel that it is a little presumptuous to propound such rules, even if they only attempt to describe a personal view of life. I have a distinct feeling that what I am attempting to express by the word *life* is something too close for me to keep at a distance and convincingly lay down rules. The very thought of doing so makes me feel the limitations of all abstract thought, including this particular thought.

The Unity of All Living Things

An ecosophy is a comprehensive view partly inspired by work on solving the ecological crisis. The word *ecosophy* is composed of the prefix *eco-*, which comes from the Greek word *oikos*. It may be translated as "household" and can be understood as the very basis of life on earth, the ecosphere. The root *-sophy*, from the Greek *sophia*, stands for wisdom. Ecosophy therefore concerns wisdom in relation to the foundation of life on earth. Ecology as a science does not say what we shall, must, or should do. Hence ecosophy does not have an exclusively ecological foundation. Ecology defines demonstrable hypotheses about what actually happens in the richness and diversity of life on our wonderful planet. But it does not specify conservation. From a purely scientific point of view, it is quite interesting to observe peculiar new changes caused by gigantic human enterprises.

What is now required, in the first place, is not so much to collect even more data on the effect of human activities on climatic change, for example, as to take more seriously the saying "Better safe than sorry." To demand *proof* that such changes will occur reveals an untenable concept of what data and theory can deliver. What we need is a more intense focus on understanding and wisdom. Given that, we can act decisively now, and that is what we need—not excuses for procrastination. There are different ways of articulating an ecosophy or part of it. That we each have our particular way does not mean that it is simply our own. Even if we use a language in a unique way, by no means is that language determined exclusively by us; rather, it is necessarily rooted in social and cultural conditions.

What is central to a person's ecosophical outlook is the demonstration of that which we consider to have a *profound meaning* in life, an understanding of the warp and weft of tapestry. The ecosophy that I have sought to expound I call ecosophy T ("T" for Tvergastein, my hut on the Hallingskarvet Mountain in Norway), while others will formulate their views in their own particular way, ecosophy A, ecosophy B, and so on. The deep ecology movement consists of just as many ecosophies as there are supporters. There are emotionally decisive variants, where the intensity or strength of the universal aspect is concerned. An ecologically oriented friend, the author Warwick Fox, has put it approximately in this way: "I feel like a leaf on the tree of life." But to me this seems a far too close relation between leaf and tree. I feel more of an individual than would be allowed to a leaf. I feel more like a little tree in a huge forest.

If I feel that something is alive, I feel that somehow it has a basic resemblance to myself. For some years this feeling persuaded me to declare that fundamentally, all life is one. In a television debate in the early 1970s, my formidable opponent, the English philosopher

Sir Alfred Ayer, found this proposition shocking. He was sorry that *I*, who was otherwise such an empirically minded and reasonable philosopher, could maintain anything like this.

Today, a leading responsibility of humankind is the responsibility for future generations; that we hand down a planet with resources as great as we found in our own generation. But we also have a responsibility for future living creatures in general. This is a fundamental ecosophical subject with its own periodicals and teaching. These concerns are not an abstract responsibility. We think of future landscapes, and our imagination helps us to dwell on different possible changes. Many people today have an unpleasant feeling that our environmental policy is discounting the future. Every day there is less space for the next generations of both human beings and other living creatures.

Let us look a little more closely at situations in which we must choose between satisfying our immediate needs on the one hand and, on the other, the fulfillment of something desirable in the near or distant future. Not surprisingly, we most often choose the present rather than the future when time is the only distinction. When the choice concerns a certain degree of greater fulfillment in the future or something less immediate, what is the exact point at which we switch over to making the decision in favor of the future and long term?

It is obvious that the decision is connected with strength of feeling. It takes time for children to learn to wait for something good instead of choosing something immediate that is perhaps somewhat less good. There is a similar problem when it is a question of choosing between an immediate, mild unpleasantness or deprivation and an intense future unpleasantness and deprivation. How much worse must the future prospects become in order for us to accept willingly an immediate but slightly unpleasant deprivation?

The question arises in all forms of conserving natural resources. Extremely high-lying, steep, precious arable land in the Himalayas is protected against erosion by shrubs. If, for example, the shrubs are used for heating water to give tourists warm showers, those who cultivate the land will enjoy instant earnings. The removal of such an income may be awkward at the time. But the alternative is much worse. When there are no longer any shrubs to contain the flow of water, erosion becomes stronger and stronger, and the topsoil will be washed away. The loss of the arable land will mainly lead to greater discomfort for those who live there. A conflict arises between those who want to stop the destruction of the shrubs and those who deliberately take the risk of continuing to use them up, or are thoughtless or somewhat irresponsible.

When Westerners point that out, the answer often runs something like this: "Mind your own business. Don't try to replace the old colonialism with a new, ecological kind." Clearly Westerners ought to *cooperate* with ecologically inclined local people to a greater degree. Large numbers should stay in the affected areas longer than they normally do. On returning to their own, prosperous countries, young people ought to be offered work in the field of foreign aid.

What Exactly Is a Feeling for Nature?

Throughout history we in Norway have had a wide spectrum in our emotional attitudes to sea, mountain, forest. Archeological and written sources bear witness to this. The location of houses has been determined not only by a need for protection against wind and weather. It was also important to have a satisfying view over an attractive landscape. By and large, positive emotions have played a leading role in the choice of a home. Obviously the fear of landslides, avalanches, and other apparent dangers has also affected the location of buildings.

We need to expand the subject of feeling for Nature. As a point of departure, it may be useful to consider the word *Nature*. What does it stand for? It is all too easy to believe that it stands for a certain concept, "Nature," common to people in all epochs. In fact, the usage of the term varies widely. Most cultures do not by a single word express anything in the way of what I, and other proponents of deep ecology, have called Nature. Many translations of foreign texts use the word *Nature* by virtue of conventions that are misleading. When *Nature* appears in a translation from ancient Greek, it might stand for *physis,* but that word obviously does not express the same shades of meaning as the Norwegian word *natur* or the Latin *natura.* In translations from Sanskrit, *prakriti* might well mean the same as we sometimes mean by *Nature,* but in very special cases a fundamental meaning is "the unprocessed" in distinction to what is processed or beautified.

To invoke the word *Nature* is one thing. But we must also investigate the attitudes people have had specifically to regions that are more or less untouched by human beings. In the poetry of various cultures there is to be found an expression of strong positive feelings toward that which we call Nature, particularly wild Nature, but angst and revulsion are also present. Plato was worried about the destruction of the forests in his surroundings. Even in ancient China there were conflicts between those who wanted to keep certain areas untouched and free from human activity, and those who wanted to exploit them. In China and India there are a number of holy mountains.

In China it was meritorious to reach their summits; in India the attitudes were mixed. According to some Hindu religious leaders, it was sacrilegious, like climbing churches. In a word, wild, imposing Nature evoked a variety of culturally significant attitudes, not only fear or abhorrence.

There is some truth in the belief that most Norwegians have a strong feeling for Nature. Since they use the word mainly about what they conceive as "untouched," nonexploited Nature, I write the word with a capital *N:* Nature. But how are we to describe a feeling for Nature? Naturally, and luckily, I may say, we cannot agree on a particular answer. We talk of a "feeling for Nature" as an expression of different concepts. I will begin with a tentative definition: a feeling for Nature is a positive feeling for areas that are not obviously dominated by human activity. I insert the word *obviously* because we must admit that today all places on earth are affected by human beings, the Antarctic not excluded. It is a common Norwegian idea that one goes *into* Nature rather than *out* to Nature. One wants to find oneself, have time to think—better understand what one really wants. Some want to die a dignified death in Nature. Everyday life is often strongly marked by external pressures from different directions, not infrequently clashing with one another. In this way everyday life often makes people *beside* themselves. As a result, there may arise a longing for surroundings where one may have a clearer feeling of who one really is.

In Norway we do not have Nature worship in a religious sense with complex rituals, as we know them from anthropology. But one dresses up one's feeling for Nature in words that can obviously be classified as Nature worship. This applies to mountains. In many cultures there is a tendency for the worship of the gods to take place in the mountains, partly from ideas of the mountain as a link between heaven and earth. But we also find records of people going "into" Nature to find themselves, right back, for example, to King Nala in the Indian epic *Bhagavadgita*. It is said of his wife that, depressed by his having left civilization, she went into the deep Himalayan forests to find him. There is a beautiful prayer of hers to the highest mountain. She begs the mountain for help to find King Nala, who left her in despair. The adjectives she uses in addressing the mountain are the same used by present-day people with strong positive feelings toward mountains: dignified, noble, grand, all-seeing, elevated, and friendly.

When the environmental crisis was first seriously treated as a social and political problem in the 1960s, a divide in the view of Nature made its appearance. On the one hand there were those who considered that the value of Nature was exclusively to serve the ends of humankind in a narrow sense. On the other hand there were those who ascribed to Nature its own value, an intrinsic value, independent of the uses to which people wanted to put it. These people felt that macadamizing places of which they were desperately fond affected them personally in a way that destroyed something within them. They felt deeply attached to a place.

At the beginning of the 1980s, there was a protest movement against a hydroelectric scheme on the Alta River in northern Norway. During one of the demonstrations a young Lapp, asked by one of the police why he was there, replied, "The river is a part of myself." The motto of the Alta demonstrations was telling: "Let the river live!" The whole ecosystem was meant, including people, but the ecosystem was symbolized by the river. Feelings may also be such that there is a meaning in doing something for a living creature, however "lowly" it may be. That is to say, we do something for that living creature exclusively for its own sake.

One more example: *Eutreptiella gymnastica* is a microscopic organism that may be called a plant but, because of its movements, may also be called an animal. I once saw such an organism through my microscope in a little raindrop. It moved around the droplet like a ballet dancer. But the droplet quickly began evaporating. The movements became stiff and less graceful. It made sense to me to save the organism for its own sake by hurrying to fetch more water. I did not believe that the organism had the capacity to suffer. But I believe I might call this identifying with a living creature, even if it was one that was considerably different from myself. I felt like a luckier colleague of this organism—if very much the worse dancer.

Perhaps my attitude to *Eutreptiella* is ridiculous, but in the telling I have an opportunity to emphasize the personal aspects of an ecosophy. Some followers of ecosophy are not interested in anything but living creatures very close to us human beings. And naturally one can be an enthusiastic hunter, a meat eater, and so on even if one moves with care and thought in natural surroundings and treats other living creatures with respect. What is common to ecosophies is that their followers have a comprehensive view, and the content of the particular ecosophy reveals that one is taking account of the environmental crisis that we feel is threatening. If I am going into my own ecosophy so thoroughly, it is partly to inspire the reader to articulate fragments of his own ecosophic view. It entails value judgments and a clearer appreciation of one's own principles and emotions.

According to ecosophy T, it is obvious that human beings do not have the right to reduce the richness and diversity of life—except to satisfy vital needs. *Fundamental* needs are those that maintain life, while *vital* needs go further, to that which gives life its deepest meaning. A good motto is "Extended care for nonhuman beings, deepened care for human beings."

However, there are many who believe that if we show consideration for living creatures other than human beings, we cannot avoid neglecting human beings. It has even been said that an extended care for other creatures is a kind of denigration—a hatred of human beings. But in that case it seems as if one imagines that care is something found in a kind of bottle of a given size. If one doles out care to creatures that are not human, a little less will be left in the bottle for human beings. Absurd!

It *is* possible to extend care, reinforce it, and cultivate it. Care is not constant or immutable. It is for that reason that I have proposed the motto "Extended care for nonhuman beings, deepened care for human beings." The latter is a reminder that there are people living in completely unacceptable destitution, not only ordinary poverty. Everywhere there is deprivation that *must* be eradicated, for example, when children are dying of hunger or are permanently maimed as a result of starvation and malnutrition. Such deprivation is quite simply unacceptable. All countries, my own included, must help by sharing the huge costs of the international effort—in manpower and money—required to reduce this form of need. We must find people in our own societies who not only visit the particular regions, but are prepared to stay for years to work together with those who belong there and who themselves are active in the work of reform.

A Feeling for Life and a Feeling for a Place

Deep ecology is a movement that many of us support because of certain strong feelings. But it is worth noting that we rarely talk about the feelings themselves when we characterize the movement. This applies particularly to me. I have presented more or less abstract opinions, concepts, viewpoints, and formulations of how I myself see the matter. We theoreticians do not shout, beat ourselves on the breast, give sighs of longing, or fall on our knees.

It is not by chance that the characteristic basic terminology of the deep ecology movement does not mention feelings at all. There is no reference to wonderful Nature and nothing at all about Nature's harmony. In 1984, together with my friend George Sessions, I defined eight points which were designed to express in general and abstract terms what is characteristic of the deep ecology movement. With some minor revisions on my part, the points are these:

1. All living beings have intrinsic value.
2. The diversity and richness of life has intrinsic value.
3. Except to satisfy vital needs, mankind does not have the right to reduce this diversity and this richness.
4. It would be better for human beings if there were fewer of them, and much better for other living creatures.
5. Today the extent and nature of human interference in the various ecosystems are not sustainable, and the lack of sustainability is rising.
6. Decisive improvement requires considerable changes: social, economic, technological, and ideological.
7. An ideological change would essentially entail seeking a better quality of life rather than a raised standard of living.

8. Those who accept the aforementioned points are responsible for trying to contribute directly or indirectly to the realization of the necessary changes.

The eight points are based on the principle that every living creature has its own intrinsic worth, and the same applies to natural wealth and biological diversity. These eight points are motivated by a philosophy of life or religion from which they can be derived. To some people, the word *alive* embraces more than the biological sense alone. Hallingskarvet is the only mountain that I feel to be alive. I had a proof of this attitude when I once saw that an extremely long line of green-painted poles had been put out to prevent imbecile tourists from falling down the precipices in winter. It was clear to me that these poles offended Hallingskarvet's *dignity*. As mentioned before, during the conflict over the Alta River, we invoked the admirable motto "Let the river live!"—exactly as if a river also had a life of its own. The admonition applied not only to the river itself, but also in the sense of a complex ecosystem where the reindeer-herding Lapps also had their place. We never heard people saying, "A river cannot be alive."

For my part, the idea that all living creatures have their own intrinsic value derives from a form of intuition. If we are to answer the question of what kind of intuition this is, we are forced to include considerations of a wide range of emotions. To me, the attitude is different when the matter concerns whole species of living creatures. I do not feel that they have their own intrinsic worth, even if it is incontestably more important to preserve them rather than a single individual in the interest of the earth's richness and diversity. Classifications are abstractions and as such have no intrinsic value. The rejection of the value of emotion appears when it is objected this way: You say "felt intrinsic worth," but do the individual creatures really have their own intrinsic value?

Another vital aspect of the deep ecology attitude is the *feeling for a place.* In the past, people have had, and many still have, strong positive feelings for the place where they feel that they belong. Today many in the deep ecology movement try to stimulate a feeling for the district in which they are living. They also try to awaken such feelings among the next generation. This is called bioregionalism.

In December 1988 a rubber latex collector in Amazonia was killed by someone buying up forest. Attention was drawn to the fact that those who lived in the rain forest *without* destroying it were regularly being killed or driven out by intruders who wanted to fell the trees for timber and cultivate the land. The man who was killed considered the tree that he was tapping to be his own living tree. He and his friends were fond of the trees, which gave them an income and a means of survival. "Human beings also belong to the rain forest" is an important principle. But naturally the population density in a forest is limited. Today people are moving into uninhabited regions of a rain forest in Australia, but it is clearly on the forest's terms, not those of industry. People are preserving the forest and are in reality upholding its well-being by reducing the spread of diseases. Nowadays a forest needs human inhabitants who devote some of their time to its management. Thus in the long run human beings can be of use in improving the conditions of life on earth.

A criticism of the political relevance of the deep ecology movement is that ecosophy is only a matter of feeling. On the basis of certain feelings, its followers form a pressure group among so many other pressure groups. This is undoubtedly so, but why should we interpret it as a criticism of some kind? In that case, surely it is also a criticism of the Salvation Army? Admittedly both are groups exerting pressure, but in the same sense as other groups that are trying to realize something greater than their own well-being. It should not be held against them that they are motivated by strong feelings for the place in which they are living. In a word: We need not only to think differently about Nature, but also to act and feel differently. Political changes require emotional changes within ourselves. The deep ecology movement takes its point of departure from a philosophy of life, or more precisely in the fundamental premises of our choice of action. These may be of different philosophical or religious kinds, but common to them all is that they have respect for Nature.

Emotions Can Create the Motivation for Change

Early in the 1970s, when I wrote an article called "The Shallow and the Deep, Long-Range Ecological Movement" in the philosophical periodical *Inquiry,* my point of departure was above all a strong feeling for nature and against the constant, increasing attacks on it. It is in untouched Nature that life can develop freely, and where I myself feel free. The article was short and abstract, but it came from the heart. Perhaps it is on that account that it has spread so far and been read by so many. But it is not easy to write from the heart. For it is often difficult for words to inspire, since they must be words that penetrate emotional life—quite simply words from the heart. To find the "feeling" in our life is extremely important if we are to produce a motivation for change in the direction of deep ecology. To support such a change wholeheartedly comes most easily if one feels enthusiasm for the creative power of Nature. That something like life on earth has arisen is a miracle.

For my part, I feel that in a certain sense Hallingskarvet Mountain is living and friendly. Some people will call this a myth, which in fact is actually a very good definition. What is bad is that in our civilization the word *myth* has come to have a pejorative ring. The truth is that we sorely need to nurture our mythlike imagination. Hallingskarvet is not alive in the biological sense, even if there are many living creatures there.

In many cultures, some mountains are considered to be living; a few, divine. In the Sherpa districts of Nepal, the inhabitants regard the mountain we now call Gaurishankar as a goddess. Her name is Tseringma, which means "the mother of the good, long life." In fact, myth building has generally been almost infinitely rich. Among children myths spontaneously arise. Luckily it seems that our form of civilization does not impede the formation of myths. But myths are rarely taken seriously when children are growing up. However, they can find a home in poetry. Or rather, since poetry is a recognized literary form, there is a tendency to wrap mythical concepts in poetical clothes. We can therefore call this form *mythopoetic.*

In my case, the poetical side of my upbringing was weak. I had an unjustified aversion to language, because it seemed to compete with music. Besides, it seemed as if my passion for abstract and logical subjects dampened my need for poetry. The romantic side of my nature was satisfied by music and experience of Nature.

A spontaneous experience in everyday life rarely gives rise to strong feelings and deep thoughts. In the way that I use the word *experience,* there are so many of them. Something is happening the whole time. Let us imagine that when we turn on the television, we hear an orchestra playing "da-da-da-daaa," that is, the opening phrase of Beethoven's Fifth Symphony. Even if the symphony is relatively unfamiliar, the spontaneous experience will be richer and more complex than if someone heard similar notes arranged in a different way, "da-da-da" for example, or "daa-da-da." That first little phrase in the symphony gives the connoisseur an experience that is related to the whole symphony, or at least the first movement. For someone familiar with the symphony who has recently heard a poor performance, "da-da-da-daa" will give a bitter aftertaste somewhere "within" the experience. On the other hand, for one who heard it together with one's lover, some of that will be "within," not merely as an association with the notes, but just as spontaneously.

What we experience spontaneously is much richer than the ways we express it. A poet, on the other hand, has practice in expressing it in his language—elaborating it without abandoning the particular experience on which he is concentrating. The poet is in a position to fix the experience in our consciousness.

To See Oneself as Something More than Merely Ego

As human beings, we have an extraordinary capacity or potential to go beyond that which is good for our ego, something that seizes only a little bit of our personality. In companionship and through friendship we fulfill our human potential in a way that greatly extends our horizon. I have written above about self-realization as related to ecosophy T. Merely by extending one's care beyond one's own ego, one fulfills more of oneself. The Lapp who, during the Alta protest, said, "The river is a part of myself," was identifying with something much bigger than his ego.

When we derive some rules from those that lie deeper within ourselves, we must stop somewhere. We stop at that point which seems deepest to *us*. Here I am referring to deepest in a logical sense. Rule A is logically deeper than rule B, if B can be logically derived from A. With A as the premise, B follows as the conclusion. I have long believed, and still believe that the principle of "Self-realization!" is the logically deepest principle. At that point, for my part, the long chain of deriving rules ceases. Any other rules that I need, I try to derive from this. But when we make decisions in a serious matter, rules are naturally not enough, and we want a great deal of information on the subject. We need "facts."

My choice of the particular principle of "Self-realization!" stems partly from the fact that I am receptive to much philosophy both in the West and the East. Also it is due to the phrase's being common in everyday speech. It *can* easily be interpreted as a kind of ego trip, or as a consequence of egocentricity. Therefore I hasten to add a number of propositions about the ego, self, and Self. The self with a small *s* is the so-called social self. When people ask, "What are you?" the answer is usually what you are within society. But there is something that deserves the name "the great Self." That embraces everything with which you identify. To identify in this way gives emotional reactions in the domain of sympathy and empathy. A process of identification is created by the very fact of your feeling something of yourself in something else. Not that it need resemble yourself, but there is something about it that you recognize in yourself. Is it perhaps the life force, or that part of God that lives in all that is living—the principle of creation? Whatever it is, it is something that becomes a part of yourself, or more correctly of "the great Self." Suddenly we can identify with an indoor plant that is starting to wither, and think: Why should we throw plants away simply because they have become a little ugly? We don't do so in the case of human beings. I myself can feel like a plant and am glad that there are those who appreciate me in spite of my advanced age and decrepit appearance.

Those who support the deep ecology movement are expected to feel that the life and death of living creatures affect them in such a way that the feeling of interdependence is connected with their own philosophy of life or religion. They identify with that which is living—however different they may be from the creatures with which they identify. Such identification requires feelings, and it is easier for me to have positive feelings for the individual living creatures than for a species—that becomes too abstract. Who does not feel pain on seeing an animal suffer? In this case an emotional tone is involved. An animal's pleasure releases pleasure in a person who "sees" that pleasure. A textbook of animal husbandry from the 1930s says of pigs that one who has seen a pig's pleasure on being scratched behind the ear cannot stop scratching it every morning. The action is prompted without more ado, and the spontaneous experience one has from the reaction of the pig may accurately be described as *seeing* a pleasure.

Thus it is not only in human relations that sympathy is aroused. We human beings have a special quality in that we can also easily identify with other kinds of living creatures. Through this type of identification, we recognize something of ourselves in the other creature, or something of the other creature in ourselves. It gives an extended understanding of ourselves. And in a biological sense, that with which we identify can be enormously different from ourselves.

One aim in nature conservancy in general is to spread a view of human beings that makes it *natural* to regard other living creatures as genuine fellow creatures with a need for self-development.

Emotional development is involved here, together with the social conditions for such development. Besides learning about humans as spiritual creatures who ought to distance themselves from all that is animal-like, we ought to learn about animals as social creatures. We ought to learn about the similarities between human beings and other living creatures, about crocodiles, for example, and their care of their eggs and offspring. It is easy enough to describe the deep-lying differences—the unique talents of humankind—but what about the eagle's ability to seize, the leopard's speed, the elephant's strength, the dolphin's intelligence, the owl's sharp vision and the cat's agility? It is important that we understand from an early age the unique talents of other species, and that we develop a sense of responsibility when we interfere in their lives. The benefits are mutual.

In human relations today, there is one universal precept which is particularly important, namely, that we ought to arrange our lives in such a way that others can also live like us, if they so wish. Here I have in mind the waste and overconsumption of the West. This makes it impossible to raise everybody today up to a Western standard of living. Obviously this requires of us an increased feeling of responsibility and a felt closeness to "the others," however far off they live in hunger and abject need. But without diverting our attention from human suffering, we ought to be able to extend such concern to include the sufferings of other living creatures, especially those that are a result of human activity.

In psychology, biology, and philosophy, expressions like self-development, self-fulfillment, and, not least, self-preservation play an important role. All living creatures try to fulfill themselves. A leading hypothesis of ecosophy T is that our self-fulfillment depends on theirs, because we have the capacity of seeing all living creatures as a part of the world we share. We depend on one another, but even if such a dependence can be oppressive from time to time, it is also pleasurable; we are not alone. We often hear that people, the elderly in particular, are afflicted by loneliness, and that those who acquire pets, or a little garden, feel a sense of renewal.

It is not many years since the splendid motto "Think positive!" suddenly became widespread. "Feel positive!" is less suitable—perhaps because it resembles an order, where orders do not belong. Feelings are something that quite simply cannot be produced on demand. Great optimism is easily associated with naiveté, immaturity, and even stupidity. "He is so ridiculously stupid to believe and feel that . . ." On the other hand, pessimistic pronouncements, especially about the future, are taken as a sign of realism. Pessimistic opinions seem more intelligent. What can the reasons be? Some people will say that since great human events generally go wrong it *is* naive and stupid to be optimistic. But in the first place, *optimism* applies to developments in the long run. I often mention the twenty-second century as the time when my optimistic belief in the solution of the ecological crisis will be realized. The reason is that the aftereffects of many types of environmental damage will continue to have an effect in the twenty-first century. It is reasonable to assume that the global market will become much stronger in the times that are approaching, and compared with today that may easily lead to a doubling of trade over twice the distance. Increased strain on ecosystems will consequently be unavoidable. It is therefore absolutely necessary for the environmental movement to think in terms of centuries but continually stress what is to be done *now*.

Among the Iroquois tribes of the northeastern United States, there is the concept of "the seventh generation." That means that in considering present thoughts and actions, we ought to think of the seventh generation back in time and the seventh generation ahead. Even if it can be too facile to point to words of wisdom from a Native American society, this is an example of long-term thinking that we might need in the West.

6 *How Does Our Emotional Life Mature?*

A significant part of emotional maturing lies in converting negative feelings to positive ones. In such a process of maturing we become more conscious of which values in life are fundamental for us. This makes it easier to set priorities. Maturing does not, however, imply that we must rein in or moderate our emotional life—rather, we must make it more accessible and raise it to a conscious level for ourselves. I think that one aim must be to be able to characterize one's actions as beautiful rather than as obligations. Exposure to conflict can help to advance emotional maturing. Mastering conflicts in a mature way seems to require exposure to conflict at an early age. In this field children occasionally outgrow their parents.

The word *maturing* is well suited to the subject on which I now want to concentrate. My point of departure lies in situations where I consider my own or someone else's reactions immature. For example: "It was immature to become so angry over something so insignificant" or "It was immature not to react unequivocally against what he said" or "It was immature of you to get married" or "It was immature of you to put children into the world" and so on.

To characterize an attitude or an action as mature is something that we do much more rarely. Might this perhaps be because immature actions are more obvious than mature ones? On the other hand, we often say things to one another like "What she went through made her a much more mature person" and "He proved to be surprisingly mature for the job." If we were to investigate the frequency of the words *mature* and *immature,* it would not surprise me if we found the latter five times more often than the former. It is so much easier to give examples of immaturity and find ways of reducing it than to discuss maturity—because, after all, immaturity is a very human phenomenon.

In discussions of maturity, emotions of one kind or another are nearly always involved in the background. Spinoza writes about humankind's path to maturity of emotional life as the road to freedom. We find in him a concept that helps us when we think of our own path through life. He talks about maintaining an "own being," in the original Latin *suo esse.* He says that as our degree of freedom increases, so does our own being. Considering this development gives us pleasure. A reinforcement of "one's own path" is dependent on the transformation of passive emotions to active ones, and this happens in different ways for different individuals.

Maturing Concerns Our Entire Emotional Life

If someone changes a negative feeling like envy, for example, to friendship, we may say, "That showed maturity." But such detached cases of mature actions need not necessarily be part of a greater process of maturing in emotional life. Maturing of emotional life is a kind of change that in the long run moves the *entire* emotional life in a positive direction.

Let us begin by discussing the phenomenon of changing emotions. The wealth of emotional change that the mind undergoes in the course of a single day is incomprehensibly great. If asked, we would normally not be able to count more than a dozen instances of this kind. We would admit that we could not remember exactly. It would be a little more realistic to ask about the changes in the course of a dinner, a walk, or a film. Or we may consider the alterations in an exchange of views that, step by step and by imperceptible degrees, turns into a quarrel. There is every reason to shrug one's shoulders if one is asked about which emotions, and how many, change in a particular interval of time. We are used to answering questions about how many sat down to a meal or how many times one yawned or nodded off during a lecture. Here it is a matter of counting something that is easy to identify. We are taught to carry out many such calculations, to make surveys, and to express so many things in figures, but what has such quantifying got to do with emotions? By and large, is it not destructive to "analyze" emotions? But surely we can attempt to describe them? There seems no way round.

The situation changes to a certain extent when a person has undergone a degree of maturing in his emotional life. Maturing is usually a slow process, even if deeply disturbing events may cause more or less sudden changes. Children who lose their parents may suddenly have a new, heavy responsibility for their lives. We will find them moving a step upward in the scale of maturity. In order to avoid too much theorizing, I would urge you, gentle reader, to try to recall situations where you have delivered the judgment "That was immature!"—or where others have said something similar about you. And here it is important to consider examples not only of the emotions being explicitly mentioned, but also those relating to attitudes. It may concern racism, immigrants, or deciding whether someone is mature enough to put children into the world.

Maturing of the emotions often requires a commitment related to the transition from passive feelings, where only greater or lesser *parts* of ourselves may be involved, to active feelings, in which case all or most of ourselves is concerned. *Mature,* in my sense of the word, cannot be replaced by *adult.* Children can become what is called precociously mature, especially under the horrible conditions of concentration camps or refugee camps. They act in a way that people otherwise do only after a long-drawn-out process of maturing. Children who are suddenly required to care for younger brothers and sisters and assume responsibility in a crisis can suddenly develop a degree of maturity at a lower age than those with less responsibility. Sporadic instances of a feeling of responsibility are not enough.

The Maturing of Emotions: Seeing One Another as Subjects

In the process of maturing, we become more aware of the values that are fundamental and charged with emotion for us. We see which values we put above others, on the basis of our feelings when we have to make difficult decisions.

Let me give one or two examples of a feeling of responsibility where a change in a negative and positive direction is concerned. A six-year-old in a tram observes that his parents have to give away some money to pay for a ticket. If there is a conductor on the tram and the journey is quite short, his parents may perhaps have to go up to the conductor to obtain their tickets. Why not leave the tram without tickets? Why not try to avoid buying tickets? In Norway it is not difficult to explain that it costs money to maintain the tram, and the tramlines and everything else that is necessary to make public transport function. It is reasonable that those who use the trams pay at least a part of what it costs, in any case more than those living in parts of the country where there are no trams. Fair distribution in the abstract is difficult to grasp, but children are much concerned by what the concept actually means in practice. Everything that has to do with an advantage must be equitably assigned. Little Peter makes absolutely sure that little Paul does not receive more, that Paul is not promised more or given more consideration than he. Among siblings the distribution of good and bad is of central concern. Therefore a teenager must be able to see that the costs of building tramlines and the trams themselves must be shared among the users. To travel for nothing would be immature. Nonetheless it can become something of a game to dodge paying the fare without being caught.

Social patterns and rules are internalized within us. They are a living part of us, and we feel them to be our own without necessarily being conscious of them. In concrete cases we can easily distinguish three stages of maturity in the application of rules. I have used tram fares as an example. Either one is tempted to evade payment, or one takes care to overcome the temptation and pays. Or as a third possibility, one might not even be tempted at all. In this case, one pays as a matter of course, almost as if one had introduced the rule oneself. At one level of maturity, one is tempted into shoplifting and falls for the temptation. At the next level one is tempted but manages to resist. At the third stage one feels no temptation at all. Children who are normally socialized generally achieve the third level before school age, learning to ask their parents to buy things for them rather than simply taking what they want. The more people who do not attain the third level, the more transport enterprises must allow for their losses in what they charge—or what it would cost to install a complicated surveillance apparatus.

What about the complaint that the fares are too high? There are those who advocate not paying at all. If enough people refuse to pay, the company will be forced to lower the fares! A more mature reaction might be to ask for the company's annual accounts. A short summary is sent, with a promise of fuller information if required. In this case, the mature person behaves as a member of the community and not like some irritated teenager.

In my view, the three stages give a simplified image of three levels of emotional maturity in our social intercourse. At the same time it is a learning process. I am particularly interested in the emotional component: urgent desires, felt temptations, a feeling for others as fellow human beings, identifying with one another. The process of maturing means regarding others as people with needs and feelings similar to one's own.

The Process of Maturing Does Not Mean Diminishing the Influence of Feelings

In this context it is tempting to look at literary characters. I have chosen one of Henrik Ibsen's later plays, *John Gabriel Borkman*. The eponymous hero is a disgraced bank manager who has been to prison for fraud. The plot centers on the conflict between two women close to him: his unforgiving wife, Gunhild, and her twin sister, Ella Rentheim. Ibsen makes his characters reveal twenty to thirty negative emotions including, among others, hatred, distaste, envy, greed, craving for power over others, and frigidity. It makes sense to quote an exact number only if we clearly delimit a *concept* of "negative feelings," something that would require us to discuss a number of philosophically relevant problems. For example, can we count the feeling of power as a real, specific feeling? Or is it quite simply an unspecific pleasure released by the consciousness or the assumption that one has power over someone or something? If it concerns power over the behavior of a hunting dog, is that a negative feeling? Is the craving for power a feeling of its own—like shame, for example, or fear of water, or claustrophobia? In philosophical literature, like that of Spinoza, most feelings may be traced back to a few fundamental types.

In the case of *John Gabriel Borkman*, it is worthwhile noting the great number of references to negative feelings. They dominate. Ibsen emphasizes different variations. He does not do so with regard to positive feelings. Naturally, he refers to love, but the variety is thin and somewhat trivial on the positive side. Generalizing somewhat, I consider that the main character, the bank manager John Gabriel Borkman, and his wife seem to have stronger negative feelings than positive ones. Positive feelings, on the other hand, seem to dominate in the life of the real heroine of the play, Ella Rentheim—at all events they are noticeably strong in difficult situations. Ibsen writes in a way designed to make the reader completely believe in Ella's honesty and ethically conditioned motives. For who is it who takes care of John Gabriel and Gunhild Borkman's son with warm feelings and a warm heart? By Ibsen's standards, and those of his times, John Gabriel's fraud and five years' prison sentence were deeply degrading. He lost his friends; he lost "everything." But Ella's love was of such a kind that she could genuinely and steadfastly say that she would help him with all her power when he came out of prison: "Believe me, I would have borne it so happily with you. Shame, ruin—I would have helped you to bear all of it—all." But at the same time she calls him unequivocally a criminal: he has committed a "dreadful, horrible crime. . . . You are a murderer! . . . You have killed the love life within me!" In a word, he had to give her up to become a bank manager. And he felt that he had to become a bank manager to obtain the power he needed to realize his plans, but one woman "can be replaced by another."

Although the variety of negative feelings mentioned in this play is in stark contrast to the rather few positive ones, the play is well suited to the examination of subtle aspects of the study of human motives. Ibsen lets his creation Borkman act ruthlessly in the pursuit of his aims. But it was not necessary to make him a rascal. Reading *John Gabriel Borkman* can be made the point of departure for practice in distinguishing a myriad of feelings and motives. And as an inspiration and exercise of imagination, we ought to propose *variations* of the presentation given by Ibsen. Naturally, it is inhibiting to admire Ibsen in a way that stultifies our critical faculties. Schools and universities should train young people to recognize that joy, sorrow, envy, warmth represent classes of feelings and are often difficult to distinguish from attitudes such as tolerance, benevolence, thoughtlessness, credulity, and so on.

Maturity does not imply *reducing* the richness of emotions. A strong negative feeling toward something in *John Gabriel Borkman* is more valuable than a weak one as a point of departure. The prospects of advance are far better. Many people desperately want to achieve a maturing of their own emotions. It is even more common perhaps to wish that the feelings of others would be mature: "That was an immature action; let us hope that he shows greater maturity in the years to come." "He has shown better judgment lately; surely it has something to do with greater maturity." Some symptoms that we consider signs of immaturity may appear in old age. In that case, understandably, we use other terminology. For example, we say that these people are diminished or show signs of senility.

So *maturity* is a positive word. Teachers should be able to recognize and appreciate signs of maturity. This probably requires changes in teacher training. I wish that my teachers had discussed my blatant immaturity. But how deeply do we go in our range of premises and conclusions when we judge something as mature or immature? Raised consciousness of, and a realistic view about, one's emotional life is a sign of emotional maturity. A distinguished Arabic philosopher says, "People never have just one motive." He comments on the tendency to answer in haste questions of one's own motives, especially when an action causes suffering in others: "My motive was solely to do something good for her, but it went wrong." Maturity implies insight—a "feeling into"—one's own emotions in real situations. One must be able to keep them at a distance. Look at them from the outside, or at least try to play the role of a neutral observer: "How would I judge my action if it were not exactly my own?" Thus we must alternate between being a participant and a spectator.

Immaturity May Be Charming

As an example, let us imagine two or three close friends, scarcely twenty years old, who have decided to go to the Orient to find traces of the Abominable Snowman—a thoroughly immature decision in the view of some people. In the first place they would not have access to the regions where there are very many stories of such a creature; and second, it was fairly obvious to most people that it was only a myth. Third, such an expedition would be extremely time-consuming. Their studies would be delayed by several months. Fourth, their budget was so tight that they would have to live in miserable conditions, which would make the journey thoroughly uncomfortable, with the risk of illness. "You don't know what you're doing," was the general opinion. Charming immaturity, say I.

As a party in the matter—in my capacity of grandfather to one of those who was going to depart—I supported the plan, to the point of calling it sensible—unusually sensible. One of my main points was my principle of exploiting as much as possible the particular qualities that characterize a particular age. My view is that when one is twenty years old in Norway or a similar society, the need for comfort is minimal. Perhaps it is somewhat greater than when one is fifteen, but definitely much less than when one is twenty-five, not to mention thirty. Therefore the principle must be, Use your minimum need of comfort to do things that cannot be considered when the need increases! I also took another theory of mine into account. Imagination and wild ideas have a greater impact when one is twenty years old than later on, and disappointment when something goes wrong is less. Criticism of the kind "You ought to have realized . . . ," "Your calculations were bound to fail" does not hurt to the same extent as a little later in life. My conclusion was that to search for the Abominable Snowman was a relatively mad and imaginative idea with great emotional appeal. Ergo: the plan was sensible! It was the opponents who were commonplace; they based their criticism on what I call fluff rationality—rationality for trivia. Even though not a single footprint was found of the unusual type that a monstrous "snowman" presumably would leave behind, in my view the expedition was highly successful.

We cannot accomplish anything without a strong (but not necessarily intense) emotional charge. We talk about durable emotions! "Tough guys" do not talk about feelings, nor do they let themselves be guided by imagination. Things are somewhat different in our times. Previously, to be fond of the mountains, for example, was not a subject to be expressed in words and analyzed. In many cases the emotional relation to mountains goes through many phases. An interesting aspect is the difference between going to the mountains on holiday and feeling that one *must* go to the mountains. In such cases, what do the mountains symbolize? Obviously it is connected with fundamental principles of the good life. Exactly which feelings are mobilized? The feeling of not being constrained by anything. In the rural districts of Norway, the mountains have provided an escape from constant observation and the necessity of keeping the rules of society all the time. In the mountains, on the positive side, one has the feeling of freedom, and being faced by challenges with which one has every chance of coping. To be in the mountains does not necessarily mean overcoming storms and trying perilous rock faces. The mountains are great, but not evil in any culture. All this means that some of us long for the mountains more than anything else.

Today one condition for realizing the highest aims of both the individual and society is a heightened understanding of the processes of maturing in emotional life. The transformation of negative (passive) emotions to positive (active) ones is clearly more difficult for those who have a pessimistic attitude toward human existence in general, and in particular toward solving problems related to war, poverty, and the environment. These are attitudes that are expressed in statements like "It's no use" or "It is only in wartime that people ask what effort is needed to attain the goal. In all other circumstances the question is rather what is convenient."

There is room for different views of the effect of extreme consumerism on our maturing processes. The consumer mentality implies that we need an inordinate amount of external stimulus, things that we cannot find in our own, inner resources. The constant novelties with which we are deluged by market forces, the one more sensational than the other, may seem distracting. Human beings' attitude to the voice of *ratio* may also be disturbed by the mentality of consumerism.

There is something called novophilia—valuing what is new, simply *because* it is new. It is the belief of many people that they must be absolutely up-to-date in how they dress, what they do, what they prefer, what they like. Throw away the old things you possess! Buy the latest! A subtle view is also needed here. There *may* possibly be new products and services that are suited to facilitating the process of maturing. Expensive information technology installations may enable children around the age of ten to steep themselves in distant cultures, to learn about peace problems, poverty, and the environmental crisis. In short, acquiring a broad perspective without neglecting small, everyday matters. Weighing up the differences between the products that obstruct maturity, those that are neutral, and those that have a positive effect on maturing naturally leads to much disagreement and uncertainty. This should not, however, prevent our facing the problems.

The maturing of emotional life implies that we attach more importance to fundamental values. We discover that some values are more important than others, that family and friends, for example, mean more than a career. We become more aware of our priorities. What is decisive is that we live a life that, in our innermost being, we want to live; this is what gives our lives meaning and substance. In this case, the adage "Know thyself!" applies with full force. Regardless of what has happened to you, there is one path that is your own. As a human being, you are a wonderful creation that it has taken hundreds of millions of years to form. As long as you live, you have correspondingly vast possibilities.

I believe many people feel that they are wasting time on activity that, by and large, does not contribute to a satisfying life— either for themselves or for society. Many people would rather work with products or processes that they believe others really need; they want to do something that grows out of the whole person. Only then would they feel happier, and when one feels happy, one would like to do more of the same. That feeling has no limits when it arises from something deep within oneself. To be with people who are emotionally mature strengthens one's own maturity.

"Beautiful" Actions

In a youthful work of Immanuel Kant (1724–1804), I have found a conceptual distinction that is of great help in appraising maturity in emotional life. It is the difference between moral actions and those that are beautiful. Kant leans in the direction of believing that an action is moral if and only if it is motivated by respect for a fundamental "categorical imperative." The categorical imperative may perhaps be defined thus: you must not act in a way that you cannot accept that everyone else should act in a given situation. Some people think it is unpleasant to see *not* twice in the same sentence, but ethics generally deals (luckily?) with few things that one ought not to do and says more about what is acceptable. Here is a variation of the fundamental ethical rule without the word *not:* You should act as if you wanted everyone to follow your rule of action. This is consistent with the previously mentioned rule, that we ought to arrange our lives in a way that assumes that, if they so wish, others can also live as we do.

If one is wholly or partly motivated by a *natural* inclination to carry out an action, strictly speaking that inclination is not morally relevant in Kant's terminology, but it is *beautiful* if it is nonetheless in accordance with the dictates of the fundamental moral law. Sheer compassion may naturally make one *inclined* to do certain morally excellent things. We might remember to say more often, "There you acted beautifully." This might encourage someone more than saying, "There you acted in keeping with the fundamental moral law" or "Good! From an ethical point of view, you acted irreproachably." Beautiful actions are based on the motivation to do what one feels an urge to do. This is stronger and longer lasting than the motivation to do what one is *ordered* to do. This holds even if it is only a sense of duty that is giving the order.

I believe that we must try to combine the preservation of Nature with humankind's natural inclination to a greater degree than previously. We must try to let people experience situations that can help to develop their inclination to appreciate Nature. But eschew moralizing! Incidentally, I forget all too easily that I am using this word in a pejorative sense, in an unnecessary way to indicate a transgression of that which you yourself consider important. In Norway, as in other industrialized countries, everything is adapted to extravagance. To live in an ecologically sustainable way in a society like ours does not perhaps demand that one be a hermit, but that one be a social deviant of an unusual kind. If one wants to try to persuade others to live a similar life, moralizing over the way they lead their lives is undoubtedly less effective than trying to give constructive guidance and pointing out the consequences of the way they are living. In the end, it seems like a relief when one gradually develops a wish to behave in ways that preserve Nature. Then we feel as if we are developing in complete freedom, and we do not feel constrained by rules imposed from outside. Quite simply, we are doing something morally right as a result of a natural impulse. In that case we are doing what Kant calls "beautiful actions."

The immense significance the transition from moral to beautiful actions entails appears in the upbringing of many people. Luckily I grew up in surroundings where pilfering and the like was unthinkable. We felt no temptation at all. If a much-wanted sweet fell from a shelf in a shop, it was retrieved and put back, or handed to the shop assistant. Quite automatically. Certain norms were internalized in us, becoming a part of ourselves. If one is tempted but nonetheless obeys the moral law, there is a tiny little struggle with oneself—or a very noticeable conflict between moral and natural tendencies. If one does not fall for temptation, one can claim a moral victory and enjoy a good feeling. If one acts beautifully, the good feeling is included in the point of departure.

> *Agatha:* I won, but it was difficult. I'm glad that I managed! I acted morally!
>
> *Albert:* Oh well, I missed the happiness you felt. But I said to myself, "You acted beautifully. You acted wonderfully." To be able to say to yourself in all seriousness, "Now you've acted beautifully"—that's good enough for me. Just think, beautifully.

On this point my theory is that it is most essential and rewarding to promote a policy that enables people to say to themselves, "Now I acted beautifully" more often than they can say, "Now I acted as duty prescribes."

Compassion for Others—and Its Limits

I myself acquired the basis for seeing compassion as an essential human quality when I was able to observe psychological suffering of an extreme and shattering kind daily at close quarters. It was in the secure ward of a psychiatric clinic in Vienna in 1935. My psychoanalyst absolutely insisted that I complete my training as an analyst, and therefore I had to have some practice in psychiatry. He persuaded the director of the clinic to let me carry out my studies at any time, day or night.

One of my patients suffered from terrible attacks of angst. She had twice jumped into the Danube, but unfortunately, she said, on both occasions she had been fished out. When I first met her, she was quite clear in her head, and without angst. But she knew that another horrible attack of angst would soon arrive. She explained that they had tried everything outside the clinic to cure her. As she predicted, the horrible attack really did come. Her shrieks could be heard far away. Sedatives? The economic crisis in Austria meant that there was enough for only one dose of medication late at night—and chiefly to protect the overworked and overstrained nurses. When I sat down next to her, she was lying in a straitjacket to prevent her making an end of herself. She was only able to utter one sentence: "Now I'm really mad." Her condition lasted for several months, but she knew that the attacks would end in the spring. In the autumn, when she suddenly had her annual bout of illness, the process started with the peculiar urge to see a particular friend, perhaps because she knew that not many weeks later she would again descend into her inferno. "Then I will jump into the Danube one night," she said, and comforted herself with the thought that she would then finally be able to stop living.

I hoped on her behalf that she would succeed, but I left Austria before she made her next attempt. I do not know what happened to her. But one can really be affected by the kind of experiences that I had in the clinic in Vienna as a twenty-two-year-old. I often have dreams and thoughts about what I witnessed there.

In Oslo more than sixty years later, I was seriously annoyed with people who said that it was difficult to find something really meaningful to do. In a lecture to the University Student Union, I said something along the lines of "Sit down next to someone in raging, unbearable angst. That means more than saving a thousand people from a lesser illness." Now there are enough sedatives available in Norway, but in some other countries the situation is undoubtedly like that in Austria in 1935.

This is perhaps a suitable place to defend those who look gloomily on their own and humanity's situation, and who are possessed of strong feelings of confusion, of despair, and of being a stranger in the cosmos and in life. I mean "defending them" in the sense that their standpoint does not generally deserve the accusation of arrogance and pessimism. In many circumstances, actively to prevent a person's taking his life can be an indefensible intrusion in the liberty of a fellow human being and a denial of his dignity.

"Today we must go and visit her," said my friend in Vienna. "She wants to take her life on Sunday by throwing herself off a cliff. We have tried everything to dissuade her, but she won't change her mind and begged us earnestly not to be with her on her last journey."

The philosopher Arthur Schopenhauer is one of the thinkers in the West who has most clearly pointed out the differences between the overwhelming and wonderful phenomenon that is life on the one hand and, on the other, what it is *to live* as a human being. For tens of thousands of people it is completely meaningless to continue living. But our culture does not have any strong tradition that easily allows a voluntary termination of life.

It may perhaps sound a little unfeeling, but I think it is useful to try to distinguish what we may call active compassion from the passive kind. I believe that it is possible to have great compassion without doing anything to realize it. If one can help those who need compassion directly without any kind of preparation, it is difficult to explain how one could remain passive. In places of need where one wades among the dead and the dying, as in battlefield, one is forced to limit oneself. But it is not unusual to meet people who obviously suffer at the thought of other human beings in horrible need but yet do nothing to contain that need. We must call this passive compassion. But then there are also people who, so far as one can make out, do not have a great deal of compassion but use what little they have to help, with small gifts of money, for example.

The Maturing of Feelings through Conflicts

During harsh conflicts at school or in society, differences in maturity will be particularly clear. The effect of the differences will then be more dramatic. The Nazi occupation of Norway during the Second World War and the subsequent settling of accounts with the collaborators are particularly suited to illustrate my observation.

On 9 April 1940, the day of the German invasion, people reacted very differently to events. One man, furious that the Germans had attacked us, collected dynamite with the intention of blowing up the buildings where the German commanders presumably had their headquarters. By great good luck he was stopped. Those who heard rumors of this plan later on thought perhaps that it was brave and revealed a particularly strong patriotism. Those who were preparing a considered, well-organized resistance to the occupying power thought that the dynamiting plan was an extremely immature reaction.

Others in the Oslo district also reacted immediately and wanted to fight the occupying power with weapons. They headed for the as yet unoccupied Nordmarka, the area of wild forest country around Oslo, to try to find Norwegian military units and armories. They had good intentions but now and then were somewhat immature as soldiers. Certain German officers (who were probably without sympathy for Hitler) thought it was immature when Norwegians attacked a heavy German tank with old-fashioned Krag Jørgensen rifles. It even got to the point when a German stuck his head out of the tank and pointed out the impossibility of the enterprise. Incidentally, it was vital for those who offered armed resistance to get into uniform. If one takes up arms against an occupying power as a civilian, one becomes what is known in international law as a *franc tireur*. According to the Geneva Convention, one must be prepared for summary execution by the regular forces if caught doing battle in civilian clothes.

What about the mediator's role in conflicts great and small? We must accept the possibility that some people have considerably more talent as a mediator than others. They can act in a way that is acceptable to all parties. The antagonists have a distinct impression that the mediators are working evenhandedly. Great maturity is needed for this. Mediators search for solutions to a conflict or try to dampen its unnecessarily crude forms of expression. Which compromises offer openings? Successful mediation processes have a capacity to transform emotions in a positive direction. But the proponents of a good cause may reject any form of mediation, and there arises what is for me the vital question whether a violent struggle can continue with the help of "militant" nonviolence, Gandhi's *satyagraha*. In contrast with pacifists, the adherents of *satyagraha* seek the core of the conflict. They try to convince their opponent of their own credibility and insight into the viewpoint of the opponent. Compromises are acceptable where lesser aspects of the conflict are concerned, but not on the principles. No one is seen as an enemy; everyone is a potential friend. This is consistent with one friend's imprisoning another. There is the well-known incident when Gandhi was put in prison and with his own hands made a pair of slippers, which he sent to the man who imprisoned him—the South African leader General Smuts. Gandhi's militant nonviolence is in the highest degree an active form of nonviolence. Its effectiveness is great, and it requires of its practitioners considerable physical and mental stamina. But it is hardly realistic to expect that the parties to a conflict will undergo a complete conversion from thoroughgoing mutual antagonism to thoroughgoing positive attitudes. This is particularly true of great conflicts of the type in which Gandhi was engaged. The question is rather to what degree personal clashes and factual misunderstandings can be removed and conflicts toned down. The nonviolence that Gandhi contributed, and continues to contribute, is known to most people. In the United States at the moment there is a debate about who ought to be named as the Man of the Century—not only the usual Man of the Year. Gandhi is a candidate. That may seem paradoxical in a century historically distinguished by arms races and wars. But even most of those who are active in *preventing* disarmament, in the West and Japan, for example, must surely accept that form of active "militant" nonviolence that Gandhi stood for and that shows the way in the long term. It has become clear, particularly among high-ranking officers, that we must constantly search for a better basis for active nonviolence and let it be a part of the obligatory military service. Soldiers in Germany and Sweden have expressed ideas in that direction. But pacifism and passivity are of no use. As Gandhi says, we must seek the center of the conflict, but without weapons.

In Norway, the more "ordinary" Alta conflict is a good example of an attempt at Gandhi-inspired communication and emotional maturing in an emotionally charged situation. As demonstrators, we tried actively and consciously to keep to Gandhi's principles. Those who supported the scheme, many farmers among them, were, understandably enough, furious with the demonstrators, who made camp and blocked the road that was to be built to the proposed dam. In this connection it is important that Gandhi's teaching of a "constructive program" be made known to the activists. Such a program means that when one directly espouses something that others consider unfair or injurious to themselves, one takes care to have a plan of action that, in a convincing manner, expresses goodwill and help to those who are injured or think that they are injured by the conflict. When an angry and outraged farmer approached us, it was our principle at Alta immediately to offer him coffee. The Norwegian mentality is such that it is difficult to reject such an invitation. We then asked him how his work was going, and if there was anything the demonstrators could do to help, like mending fences. When an argument ensued, we tried to follow the six rules for being unbiased, which I have previously described.

Being Affected by the Surroundings

Things have gone far indeed if one is able to observe people in great need and pain without feeling sympathy and a spontaneous desire to do something for them. Likewise, things have gone far if one assaults people who have not done anything horrible to oneself. But one must accept that human beings between the ages of fifteen and twenty-five may be unstable in their reaction to external events and as a result may lack some of the moral strength that most of us subsequently develop.

During the German occupation of Norway, a number of Norwegian collaborators—Quislings, as they were called, after the arch–Nazi collaborator Vidkun Quisling—proved willing to ill-treat "compatriots" under certain internal and external influences. Those who ill-treated someone would talk about their actions as "giving a hiding" or "beating up." In my view they were justified in distinguishing what they did from torture. A sociologist, Nils Christie, was the only one in Norway who, immediately after the liberation, made the cruelty during the occupation a subject of sociological investigation. He investigated the behavior of Norwegian prison guards toward Russian prisoners of war whom the German occupation authorities placed in camps in northern Norway. The authorities' own guards treated the prisoners inhumanely, and they tried to find Norwegians who were willing to become prison guards and also to act brutally. The main point, according to the occupation authorities, was to make the Norwegian guards look on the prisoners as animals, not as fellow human beings in distress. It is an interesting comment on my theme that Norwegians of a more "mature" age did not allow themselves to be influenced, but some of the comparatively young ones were brutalized.

It is only on reaching his twenties that a slow, normal maturing of a human being's whole emotional spectrum begins to take effect. If we say that the comparatively young Norwegian prison guards were emotionally immature, strictly speaking, what do we mean by this? Perhaps the most obvious thing is to say that they were very easily affected by the surroundings in which they found themselves. Under Nazi influence they underwent a profound emotional change in the direction of accepting brutality. Some of the keenest torturers were apparently quite normal people.

It was an unforgettable experience to observe how a dozen very young students rapidly *developed* in their work in "the office of missing Norwegian prisoners" immediately after the end of the war. Their work was investigating what had happened to the hundreds of prisoners who had been assumed to be in Nazi concentration camps but were not found on liberation. The police allowed these students, under my supervision, to interrogate known torturers and others who might have some information about how the missing prisoners died. Emotionally, this was a terrible strain on the interrogators— and naturally on the interrogated as well. Parents were frantically asking, "What happened to my son, what exactly happened to my son?" and the Red Cross and other organizations had no time to investigate. It turned out that most of the victims had been tortured to death or had managed to kill themselves rather than face the slow agony—it could take months—of dying from exhaustion. The young students displayed a responsible, professional attitude that was quite astonishing. I would say that they grew in emotional maturity through this intense and emotionally demanding work. Let us not underrate the very young. Not only will some of them show great heroism in battle, but others will behave in an emotionally more mature fashion than older and more experienced people.

When we move from one culture to another, judging the maturity of the emotions of a particular individual apparently seems quite arbitrary. It is necessary to ask whether a ruling ethic is only relative—depending on society or culture, for example—or whether we can talk about a basic ethic that is independent of society. More generally, are we justified in talking about absolute values and value judgments? In my view it is untenable to say that what is repulsive about certain behavior must be judged in relation to society and culture. Exactly where the limits run is arguable, but in this century Nazism and fascism in particular have made social relativism unacceptable. It is important to distinguish between ethical relativism and ethical relationism. The latter means that ethical rules are intimately related to society. But merely to describe these differences, as for example in social anthropology, does not allow us to draw the conclusion that the variations that are displayed are *equivalent*. Judgments in normative questions depend on similarities and differences. We cannot legitimately deduce how something ought to be from how it is.

There are circumstances where it is not right, often because of cultural differences, to invoke the judgment "Absolutely unethical!" Seen from the standpoint of Western democracies, women are oppressed in large parts of the Third World. I agree with that point of view. But I also believe that there ought to be *strict* rules for the means of proceeding if, as an outsider, one tries to support change. In the judgment "Ethically absolutely revolting!" negative feelings in the form of horror, revulsion, and disgust naturally play a role. In this case I adopt a Gandhian standpoint, as it might be applied to torturers: absolute and utter rejection of the actions *without rejecting the person*. In fact, there may be an obligation to approach the perpetrator and enter into Gandhian communication. Gandhi advocated training in nonviolent behavior in the midst of horrible conflicts. The risk of being exposed to violence is present, but experience demonstrates that in many cases body language and attitudes that express only positive feelings have a disarming effect under circumstances that seem quite hopeless to a neutral outsider. If only 10 percent of the heroes in action films triumphed with the help of nonviolence, I believe that it would exert a positive influence on the emotional maturing of young people.

7 *You Can Learn Properly Only What Engages Your Feelings*

In an affluent country like Norway, we need an educational system that explicitly takes more account of the emotions. We talk about education, a word derived from a Latin verb meaning "to lead forth." I say that we ought also to talk about the opposite, what I might call "induction," that is, the nurturing of innate values like wonder, creativity, and imagination. There are many subjects that are well adapted to promoting such qualities, but we must produce teachers who are allowed to be personal and given more freedom in the way they teach. Furthermore, the standards of attainment must be lowered—to learn well is to learn slowly. Teaching is only effective if pupils and students concentrate now and then on something for which they have a burning interest.

Norway is a country with a special need for promoting an upbringing and education that benefits emotional maturing. Why? We have great material wealth on account of our natural resources, and we no longer have any great, burning political conflicts. We have unusually rich opportunities to ask what we want to do with our lives. We can follow impulses and cultivate values that most people in the world can only dream about. And in fact we can afford to say to schoolchildren and university students, "If there is something that particularly attracts you, you may concentrate on that in particular and cut out much else."

Many children think it's fun to hear about dinosaurs. But they also become interested in the fact that these animals lived so long ago—and thereby, perhaps, they become fascinated by the distant past of humankind as well. A teacher can use the subject of dinosaurs to illustrate the relation between predator and prey generally, and perhaps this may be applied to questions of human society, like the use and abuse of power and violence. For my part, the proposal is intended as an example of how we might introduce at school various subjects that may be assumed to promote maturity. What we need is a kind of *education of the feelings*. This education must concentrate on developing the few but vital subjects in which children and university students are interested. In Norway we have the opportunity of changing the learning process of people between the ages of about six and twenty. We can change it from being mainly knowledge-oriented to becoming feeling-oriented as well. Burning commitment and the process of maturing ought to be central aims for young people.

Mature in One Thing, Immature in Something Else

If parents were to be what they were in times past, they would have to take several months of advanced training in changes in society and youth culture today. To be young nowadays is completely different from what it was a few decades ago. The pressure of consumerism on teenagers was relatively unknown then. The market for children's clothes is constantly expanding today. It is a marketing process that is rather important for economic growth. Parents and teachers must become familiar with this, and naturally learn about the priorities of the young. In a word, if parents and teachers really want to know and influence the world inhabited by youth, they must understand what the younger generation scorns and where its active interest lies. This often revolves around matters that are emotionally charged in a fundamental way.

Let us imagine that an inspector appears in a tram, and a teenager called Alexander, who is without a ticket, is in danger of being caught. But his friend Charles quickly gives him his own ticket. He feels that he is better able to take the consequences. Personally, it is a thoroughly mature action. But the very next day, Charles himself becomes a fare dodger. It is socially immature, since he is evading an obvious responsibility. Perhaps he is the victim of an immature ideal of cunning to be found in society today. Immaturity in one thing and maturity in something else may intimately coexist in young people. That they are anchored in the morals of the peer group is perhaps the most important cause of retarded emotional maturity among many young people. It *is* asking a great deal of parents today that they should help children in the process of emotional maturing. But at the same time, we are justified in demanding it. It is part of the responsibility of putting children into the world.

Now that I have expressed myself so forcefully about how important it is to understand contemporary youth, some people might react against my going more than three hundred years back in time to find material for the thought, but I do so just the same. Spinoza pointed at the faulty education of his own times. If upbringing were essentially better, far more people could follow the dictates of *ratio* and thus attain a greater degree of freedom in their own lives. Spinoza considered that the education of his time was distinguished by a false religiosity and the use of fear as a means of control. And fear is a passive, negative feeling that appeals to a sense of powerlessness and helplessness.

On the other hand, if parents and teachers manage to develop feelings of friendship, the way ahead is clear: those who are growing up are better prepared to join more and more inclusive circles of friends. Such circles of friends form the very foundation of a society of free humans. It is possible that Spinoza means that if parents are slaves of passive emotions, they will inevitably use negative methods of upbringing, like punishment, mockery, anger, and authoritarian rules, for example. It is obviously necessary to set limits, and children need authority, but positive authority. Otherwise, as we have seen, a vicious circle ensues. Unfree parents make unfree children; unfree children grow up and become unfree parents. The same applies to teachers. Spinoza's optimism derives from human nature's being on the side of friendliness. The development of humanity and fellowship gives pleasure, and in the long run this must benefit the process of bringing up children.

One instance of how the development of human qualities may be encouraged is through a feeling for Nature, which I have already touched upon. The attitude to Nature appears most often in childhood as something that is absolutely essential for many people. Some children are fortunate enough to have parents and teachers who show them how much they appreciate Nature, without words perhaps but by attitudes and body language that stimulate children to think and give vent to their imagination. They might perhaps begin to imitate the adults' way of moving carefully, become fond of lying on the grass, observing the movement of the clouds, and amuse themselves by watching how the moon plays hide-and-seek behind the clouds. If parents approve of and support this, it would be strange indeed if a child did not develop strong positive feelings for Nature and *all* creatures that they consider to be living. The voice of *ratio* proclaims generosity and spiritual strength, and hence all the other positive qualities, also toward fellow creatures. In this field the educational system is faced with a herculean task.

Education and Induction

What characterizes education in schools and universities in the Western world today, when compared with education in previous times, is that information is emphasized more than knowledge, and abstract subjects more than concrete. There is also the rise in the variety and volume of subjects.

Today objective or quasi-objective knowledge is given a central role. On this account people complain about objectivity in the sense of fellow human beings' becoming objects of competition and research from the outside rather than from inside, from themselves. As a result, friendship and compassion become subordinate. The *successful* person is the one who acquires importance, advances, and becomes better off and more accomplished than the majority. That is the danger of the knowledge society.

Justifiably, we accept that the development of a person's intellect is a long-drawn-out affair. This puts its stamp on education from kindergarten to final university examinations. That is to say, we consider education to be a common good, as a result of which the extensive education of members of society has a relatively important place in the national budget. But although it is important to acquire more information, more attention ought to be paid to what I might call "entertaining" or "pleasurable" material, characterized by positive emotions. Such material is found in mathematics, both in the theory and the choice of problems to solve—material that gives pupils the feeling that they are mastering the subject. "Useful" means something that develops an appetite for learning more, not only what we consider that pupils ought to know.

The Norwegian word for education—*utdannelse*—is interesting. Why the prefix *ut* ("out") was added to the older word *dannelse* is uncertain. The root of the noun *dannelse* is *dan,* which is derived from the older *dôn.* This is found in the English verb *do.* In other words, *utdannelse* meant to do something special with the development of a human being from child to adult. At an early stage the word *dannelse* acquired an association with the upper or middle class. It was also used to indicate people who behaved in a way prescribed by the rules, not least in speaking properly. In English there is no equivalent for the twin words *dannelse/utdannelse. Education* encompasses both senses. It is obvious that even this word, in the same way as the Norwegian *utdannelse,* covers vocational training to a greater degree than was the case in former times. Despite this, more has been done in England to preserve the educational aspect, in its true sense, than in the egalitarian Norwegian society.

When we try to recall how we felt about our school days, we often mention warmly a particular teacher who turned an otherwise boring subject into a pleasure. "I did like such-and-such a teacher." What can be done during teacher training to produce teachers whom pupils will quite simply like? Unfortunately, many teachers are seen by their pupils as tired and harried people. This may be the result of the teachers' own attitudes and manner of speaking. A teacher might perhaps say, "You will do badly in the exam if you . . . ," instead of, "You can do brilliantly if you . . ." What I am driving at is that we must pay greater attention to the emotional tone in the course of education. I am convinced that to feel pleasure on being introduced to a subject leads to a doubling of what one learns per unit of time, not to mention a doubling of the desire to learn more! And to have positive feelings toward a teacher also leads to a doubling of the pleasure in learning a subject, or it might even change the view of a subject from "ghastly" to fun.

This brings me back to induction. By that I mean emphasizing feelings, creativity, and imagination, which ought to be a self-evident part of all education in our society. This touches on something that comes from the heart, from emotional life. How can emotional induction be combined with education? One way might consist of putting greater emphasis on the emotionally related aspects of a subject and giving greater attention to the emotional experience of subjects pupils have while studying.

Unfortunately there are few people in Norway who are wholeheartedly working to persuade the country to adopt a *bold* educational policy—and that in spite of the fact that Norway is extremely affluent, with both time and money to focus on the emotions. We can, if we wish, grant the extra resources necessary to allow children to linger on that which fires them with enthusiasm, without their being forced into a curriculum that leads only to their becoming more and more alienated from the surroundings that others have constructed for them.

We ought to demand that some of the emotions that drive the mathematician or the musician are also cultivated and supported in the teaching of mathematics and music. I mean the feeling of being on a voyage of discovery: "Oddly enough, this can be done!" "Listen to this!" "We can, or maybe we can't, do this." Wonder and mastery can go hand in hand.

Learning and Unlearning

A word that ought to be used more is *unlearning*. All learning of new advances presupposes unlearning of something old. When something new is inconsistent with something old, the old knowledge must be erased one way or the other. If the old knowledge is felt in a particular positive way, the source of that feeling will disappear. Then the question arises, Can the new knowledge be felt in the same way as the old? If the answer is yes, we do not lose anything emotionally. But we must realize that a variety of sources dry up during early childhood without the transfer of related feelings to new circumstances, new things, or new people. This applies, for instance, to the mythopoetic sources, like the ability to regard a mountain as a king and listening to what the trees are saying. At least that is the state of affairs, unless a very special kind of teaching is adopted with the deliberate aim of preserving the mythopoetical imagination.

Many will ask, What on earth is this mythopoetical concept? The book that I published in 1995 about the Hallingskarvet Mountain, describing it as "the father of the good, long life," is considered to be mythopoetically motivated. It is quite clear to me that as a ten-year-old I contrived an image of the nature of this mountain that was clearly mythic. Perhaps the capacity to make up such myths is present in everyone at that early age, but few take the time to linger over their own mythical inventions and to continue making new ones. The surroundings in which people grow up do not promote self-confidence where imagination is concerned. As a child I often stayed in my mother's hut at the Norwegian mountain resort of Ustaoset, where I was left entirely to myself and my imagination. I discovered a foundation there for an inner life that is perhaps not granted to many children today. But the ability to create myths has hardly disappeared. All that is needed is that adults appeal to that ability at school also. Teachers ought to ask: "What are you doing in your daydreams? Wouldn't you like to tell me something about them? Or would you prefer to write about them? That might help you."

How Do We Create and Develop Commitment?

Schools and institutions of higher education face great challenges in giving emotions a place in the system. Instead of concentrating too much on so-called useful information in the form of facts, we ought to start with that which makes pupils and students *want to learn.* This requires encouragement and commitment from the teachers' side. But how much is actually done during teacher training and in the schools to make teachers into experts in giving consolation, spreading encouragement, and creating optimism? There is much complaint about laziness and apathy among pupils. But there must be a way of training teachers to fire their pupils with fervor.

Encouragement need not lead to complacency among those who are being encouraged. Luckily there are teachers like the one I had in the mathematics of the general theory of relativity. Even if in answering his questions I was wide of the mark, this teacher always exclaimed: "Precisely!" Thereafter he corrected me by presenting what seemed to be *slight* alterations to my hopelessly wrong answer.

I am often asked, "But what do you mean by fervor?" In reply I can offer what I believe are instances of the development of a fervor in everyday life, from social spheres of which I know little. In sports there are people who, from their early years, without encouragement or payment, take on onerous duties on teams or in organizations of various kinds. There are thousands of people who engage in cultural activities, in amateur dramatics, old-age centers, study circles, exhibitions, voluntary work in different art forms, preservation of cultural monuments, and the like. They become involved in long, enduring, energetic, selfless, enjoyable social and cultural work.

The expression *fervor* is particularly appropriate in the case of passionate social commitment. As an old professor, I know that there are many students who are so deeply engaged in something very specific that the term *fervor* can be applied to the force that they radiate. The spectrum ranges from a weak dark red to white heat, to use colors as an illustration. Fervor is such a powerful phenomenon that under any circumstances it rarely goes unnoticed. Surely such a phenomenon, if it is recognized, can be used to improve the teaching in our schools? But in that case both teachers and pupils must be on a considerably looser rein than is the case today. And the central authorities must be willing to let schools decide on learning projects and the final curriculum.

The question we must now pose is, What are we to do with the many people who do not feel a burning interest in anything at all, but for one reason or another still wish to study? What about the unquiet souls who are constantly flitting from one subject to another? I believe that this applies to most of us. In the first place there are obviously only a few who really are afire to the point where they persevere with a narrow specialty right through to a doctorate. More students change their interests along the way, and many finish their formal education long before they are qualified.

Feelings for Subjects

To a great extent good education is a matter of mature feelings. Is this trivial, accepted by most people? Perhaps. But what can be done to foster mature feelings, or, to be more realistic, what can be done to make it a little easier for young people to proceed on the long road to maturity? One of the many ways is to take historical examples. History tends to stress the influence of personalities. That suggests a one-sided judgement, encouraging a degree of competitiveness among the young: "I am *more* than you are." At this point the reader may well object that history cannot concentrate on the great spirits who did not exert great influence. They "did not make history."

There is a tendency to regard certain subjects as difficult and boring into the bargain. Well-brought-up pupils are reluctant to express their feelings, even if they think that the subject is vile. The point is that our kind of society provides favorable, secure circumstances for people who are energetically and constantly committed to everything that seems to be dry and intellectual. It is one of the main threads in this book that the situation can and must be changed, and that affluent countries can afford it. A suitable slogan might be "From vile learning to fun learning!"

Not enough is done to promote aspects of subjects that utterly grip pupils. Those who do what they can to absorb the curriculum have a right to access to the emotionally most challenging parts of the subjects in question. Wonder, especially pleasurable wonder, is an emotion to which more attention must be paid when students choose their subjects. In historical studies different epochs, societies, and events may arouse more or less pleasurable wonder and curiosity. The teacher can let students have more of that pleasure by observing their reactions and actively encouraging their wonder and curiosity. A class ought to be able to spend much more time on some subjects at the expense of others if it is motivated in a particular direction. The subject and the mutual relations between the pupils and between pupils and teachers can then contribute to the maturing of emotions more intensely because the pupils are allowed to cultivate their fervor.

In teaching it is possible to concentrate on excitement and drama without impairing the solidity of knowledge, while imprinting the Socratic feeling of limitation. Certain events and political conflicts are calculated to excite interest. A history teacher who puts great emphasis on economic conditions will find enough crashes, bankruptcies, unbelievable good fortune, amazing events, and so forth to use as living examples when trying to illustrate abstract economic concepts. The story of the Great Depression, from the Wall Street crash of October 1929 onward to the presidency of Franklin D. Roosevelt, is quite unique. Who can be bored by a study of this crisis? A few but not many, I would guess. One should not hide the fact that highly respected professors of political economy uttered completely wrong predictions. What kind of school and educational system would we then have? Not a school merely of knowledge. A school of emotions? Hardly. But my proposals imply a decisive, positive re-evaluation of the role of the emotions as a motivating factor in all teaching. And if we can infuse *some* with new fervor, it can help others.

If we throw a pebble into calm water, it generates circular ripples that spread quite far. A student who discovers *something* in a subject that arouses his fervor also becomes keen to learn subjects that are closely related to and support a more intensive study of this positively, emotionally charged subject. Let us suppose in a period of one year, a student is required to study ten topics in a subject. Let us further assume that of those ten topics, two arouse strong feelings of enthusiasm. As a consequence of such emotional engagement, the eight other topics ought to be reduced to a minimum at the start or, best of all, eliminated. What is rarely if ever considered is that precisely because pupils feel that they have mastered something, most of them want to *continue* with the topic or closely related ones. More than anything, they want to go deeper and farther. Since "everything is related to everything else," a teacher may broaden the scope of the discussion. "You want to go deeper into topic A. Yes, but you must then learn a little about B. Which also means a little about C. But we will not of course abandon A as our focus."

It is understandable if the reader now thinks, "Yes, that's all very well, but schoolchildren today are not what they were a generation ago. They insist on acting as individuals on the same level as the teachers." One consideration that makes things even more difficult is that in most classes there are some pupils who absolutely will not open up. They refuse to consider anything that smacks of cooperating with teachers and school. The school must not take the opportunity of meddling with their feelings. "Let us find out the minimum we can get away with in order to pass our exams and get on. We'll manage. Let us avoid any risk of personal relations with teachers and naturally any reference to our feelings! That's our own affair—we haven't asked to go to school!" These are opinions that are often heard in different guises. I admit that readers who raise this point have put their finger on a real problem. For in practice this is something that would prevent many teachers and the majority of pupils from supporting a school that was less knowledge-oriented and concentrated more on being an institution for the emotions and the process of maturing.

Michael Soulé is the founder of the so-called conservation biology movement. This maintains that biodiversity, that is to say, the diversity of species on earth, has an intrinsic value and must be protected. The richness and variety of life must be maintained as far as humanly possible. In the same way as deep ecology, Soulé's movement declares that living creatures not only are useful; they have an intrinsic worth of their own. Conservation biology has won great support among biologists in English-speaking countries. It seems obvious that the movement is kept alive by strong emotions to a considerable degree. In teaching biology one ought to cherish and develop these emotions. Humankind can presumably survive the extermination of millions of animals and plants and the macadamizing of a vast number of square kilometers, but in my view an appeal to the fear of catastrophe is not the path to follow. To preserve the variety and richness of life, it is necessary to preserve and develop the positive feelings that many people have when they choose biology either as a line of study or as a general interest. In other words, the most favorable circumstances must be realized so that the individual can develop. I have the impression that this does not occur at most highly respected universities. Introductions to biology, the science of LIFE, tend to be dry, focusing on details.

I remember vividly a week's field trip for students majoring in biology to some quite overwhelming landscape in northern Mexico. Professor Soulé and I led the trip, but it turned out that we were dealing with a flock of students who, after several years' study, seemed to have lost both intensity of feeling and the will to commit themselves. Classification and related topics were all that they concentrated on while working, but we spent most of the time enjoying ourselves. At my urging we introduced a daily hour of silence in order to absorb Nature in all its majesty. But obviously, a lack of emotional commitment could not be instantly cured. To pass an exam and finish a dissertation was far too important. I turned a large stone over and examined the life beneath it. There were hundreds of organisms that I had never seen before. Great fun! There were wonderful snakes in the vicinity, but almost predictably, I was alone in observing one.

Just imagine: biology is supposed to be a science about life, and yet the subject as a course of study has so little to do with life itself. At the very least, if students are enjoined to silence, they tend to look around. You can point something out, and they are puzzled: Surely *that's* nothing special? Well yes, that's a withered blue anemone. The root is alive. What you see is a living organism. Withered? What do you mean by that?

What about that most dreaded subject of all, mathematics? Its topics show an endless variety. Schoolchildren regard the subject with attitudes ranging from hatred to burning enthusiasm. It is culturally important to compare the mathematical syllabus down through the ages. What the system demands of students beginning their studies at the university level today would have qualified for a university chair a hundred years ago. The methods of demonstration have become more precise, and study has greatly accelerated. Previously one sauntered through mathematics; now one has to "master" everything, and do so in a shorter time than before. So everyone who has difficulties with math today ought to be told how much more they really know by comparison with people who lived a century and a half ago.

As an example, I will cite an introductory mathematics textbook that I know well. The example is so striking that it may be worth remembering, even if not all my readers like reading about mathematics. The author is Ludwig Kiepert, and my copy of his book is the fifteenth edition, published in 1923. It is a German work, of which the title, translated into English, is *A Fundamental Outline of Differential Calculus and an Outline of Integral Calculus.* The work comprises 1,909 pages, divided into four volumes. (Typically German? An outline of nearly 2,000 pages.) So are 1,909 pages daunting? No, there is no reason to be afraid. On the contrary. The work proceeds so slowly, and gives such an amazing number of examples of everything, that it can almost be read in bed like a novel. Only a few appendices are heavy going. The main thing is that we unquestionably have a feeling of mastering the material because we advance so slowly. All the proofs and formulas can be taken in stride. Reading the book now and then requires patience, but the path one follows is straight enough. Now and then one may perhaps feel superior and skip a page or some examples. But one manages the kind of exercises that are seemingly difficult, because the method is exemplified in all its ramifications. Interest is kept up, not least because of the obvious genius of the founders of calculus, Newton and Leibnitz!

A modern textbook covering the same ground has such a steep progression that instead of four volumes, one small one is enough. A great deal must simply be learned by rote, so that there is no time to develop a proper understanding. Irksome memorizing is not required when Kiepert presents the material.

Some people, if not exactly fond of numbers, are nonetheless favorably disposed to them. Through my window at Tvergastein I can now see a strip three meters long and half a meter broad, blooming with harebells. There are seventy-nine of them. Not bad at an altitude of fifteen hundred meters and sixty degrees north latitude. Some people may perhaps think that my quoting seventy-nine is somewhat ridiculous. But to others, it provides a piece of information lacking in "a whole lot" or "many." The precise figure seventy-nine is more expressive—for some of us. And the harebells are not less romantic on that account.

There are those who in early childhood find their pulse quickening when they hear strange things about enormous figures. A little boy of my acquaintance, who did not want to learn eight times seven because it bored him, was happy to learn eight times seven septillion. He liked writing out those twenty-four zeros. He felt as if he was mastering something that was almost incredible. The little point I am trying to emphasize is that an appeal to imagination and the love of the fantastic or paradoxical eases the introduction of new topics in the peculiar mathematical and formalistic way. We may well ask ourselves what is left in mathematics if the positive emotions have vanished? With computers in the home, it is difficult to establish precisely what a student really needs after completing his studies. We only know that if mathematics is introduced in an emotionally positive way, there is a receptivity to learning more.

When one of my professors at the Norwegian technical university in Trondheim wrote a famous equation on the blackboard, he had a certain body language that was overflowing with emotion. He moved quite slowly in front of the blackboard. He stared for a long time at the symbols in the formula. He whispered, as if the formula were not to be disturbed. He looked at us silently, as if he wanted to say, "Are you there?" I would scarcely advocate inculcating such behavior in today's teachers, but the effect on the listeners was great and clearly stimulated our desire to probe deeply into mathematical problems.

All the way from learning that "seven times eight equals fifty-six" through to graduation and a doctoral degree, there is every reason to make math irresistibly interesting. But a one-sided demand for mere information dilutes a sense of wonder and pleasure at something that one senses but does not understand. A student bursts out, "Ugh, I don't understand it," instead of "That's fantastic, and yet I can't understand it." It is not necessary for children to understand a conjuror's tricks. It may be entertaining to understand one or two tricks, perhaps, but the stranger the things seen by children, the greater the enjoyment. Schools and universities insist that you understand *properly*. Therefore I caused puzzlement when I wrote in an introduction to a textbook of philosophy that he who thought he had understood *everything* in the book had not understood anything.

My conclusion is that if a pupil feels that something in a subject is fun, then let him have much more of that something. Proceed so slowly that the overwhelming majority of pupils have the wonderful feeling of mastery. *Then* one can go more deeply into the subject *because* it is fun to learn. Is what I am recommending uncertain? Yes. Of course it is. I have taken things to extremes. I do not believe that I am proposing utopian ideas, but I am nonetheless open to well-thought-out compromises.

What You Want Is What You Feel For

In 1939, when I began my career as a professor of philosophy, the whole question of the nature of a university was very real to me.

What did we really want to achieve? What were our fundamental priorities at the university? What did the students think about it? What were they passionate about, if indeed they were so? The atmosphere was not such that I could expect help in finding answers. I sensed that most of my venerable, immensely learned colleagues would generally be satisfied with the status quo, whereas I found it miserable, like being back at school.

The agenda of our Wednesday faculty meetings was usually very long. The large number of minor questions of detail had priority. As a result, the basic assumptions of what we were doing were not even touched. I say venerable colleagues, since many of them were not only vastly learned, but in addition had great experience in higher education. My own ideas were doubtless romantic. And I did not properly understand that the ordinary student had a relatively limited need for active participation in shaping the teaching. They accepted an authoritarian regime.

I have sometimes been asked if I really believe that students only have a "relatively limited need" of individual attention and active participation. Yes indeed, that has been my experience. When one of my students told me that he wanted to continue studying philosophy beyond the preliminary examination, it was with high expectations that, as his professor, I asked which philosophical topics particularly interested him. I looked forward to helping him personally. But unfortunately it turned out that there were no particular questions to which he was seeking answers. He would find philosophy in general mildly "interesting"—without showing commitment to any particular subject matter.

I suggested that the students put much work into formulating their questions themselves and write down their own judgment of what they read. There are no final answers in philosophy. My reasoning was that if my students were allowed to cultivate a certain "focus," the curriculum would be reduced and concentrated on certain parts of philosophy's ocean of topics. But the majority actually wanted a broad curriculum instead of focusing on topics that they preferred. It was a part of student life to complain about cramming, but great personal initiative and a clear concept of what one wants and where one is going applied only to a minority. We must nurture this minority and offer support beyond ordinary teaching.

Given the circumstances now at many universities, study is still directed to providing students with a huge mass of information. It is, however, far more important to help students develop self-criticism, which, in its turn, requires that the teachers themselves be convincing in their own capacity for self-criticism. I have allowed students to gain their master's degree despite not having extensive knowledge. On the other hand, they were well aware of their own limitations. Great harm may be caused by the combination of much learning and little self-criticism.

To a great extent, finding one's own way consists of discovering what one really wants, and that requires much elucidation of where one's strong, lasting emotions are lodged. Something is interesting but not gripping—not heartrending, not anything one feels that one *must* probe more deeply.

Personally Experienced Problems Are the Starting Point

It was a lack of encouragement for students to articulate their own *evaluation* of things that horrified me when I suddenly became professor of philosophy, which is one reason I tried to change the preliminary examination in the years to come. This examination ought to have dealt with a small number of core topics based on historical considerations and naturally including Chinese and Indian philosophy. Philosophy knows no frontiers, but there was great opposition from the faculty members with strong views on Christianity and the history of ideas. European traditions ought to suffice, and they thought that *something* had to be said about each one of a long succession of philosophers, at least to the extent of a page or two.

In my view this was too superficial at a university level. The curriculum was insufficiently related to the philosophical aspects of the students' own personal problems. It is an elementary rule in education to start where the students stand, not with topics and viewpoints that are more or less foreign to them.

Following this rule, during the 1950s I introduced an alternative to the preliminary examination in philosophy, which I called the "ethics alternative." Before I put it into practice, I urged the students to talk about decisions and conflicts in which they were involved and which had both a particular and a general application. Male students mentioned the problem of whether they ought to agree to military service or object on grounds of conscience or nonviolent antimilitary principles. Furthermore, relations with the opposite sex were a topic that they felt ran deep, and here they received unqualified support from the female students. Otherwise, they were concerned with the relation between the morality and attitude to life of their own circles on the one hand and that of parents and society on the other. Is being an informant always objectionable? Suppose that someone in one's circle of friends commits a criminal offence. How far ought one to keep silent to prevent the action coming to the attention of parents, superiors, or the police? Are some cases so serious that one is quite simply compelled to act as an informant? All ethical topics have interested philosophers and, from a professional philosopher's point of view, I considered it quite justified to make them a central point of departure for teaching. It was natural and necessary to give the problems a historical background—but background, not foreground. What was most important was the problems themselves, not their intricate historical development.

One of the many kinds of practical exercises in the alternative philosophical course designed to train the students was the consideration of possible conflicts between the principles "Be honest" and "Be kind." Many students spontaneously said that one ought to be *both* honest and kind, and that hence there was no conflict.

Meanwhile the temperature of the discussion rose quickly. The subject of honesty versus kindness leads to the question of prioritizing values and norms. That led to questions of fundamental norms and hypotheses (axioms, fundamental assumptions)—in a word, both philosophical breadth and profound contexts and systems. All this was examined from the students' own emotionally conditioned conflicts and reflections. In this kind of context it is easy to introduce references to the established history of philosophy.

Required reading? Not much more than seventy pages! The course was directed to that which was emotionally conditioned, and answers to the exercises could themselves be characterized by intense feelings, but supported by argumentation. Put simply, I was trying to introduce students to a form of enjoyable activity centered on problems that they were in a position to feel.

Immediately after I was appointed to my chair, a Norwegian historian, Sverre Steen, warned me against asking permission of colleagues and the faculty to introduce my ethics alternative. "Do what you believe is right," was his advice. The ethics alternative would never be officially accepted. It would give the students unheard-of influence on their teaching and therefore, to raise one objection, would defy precedent, in the view of the majority. In the first term that the ethics alternative was announced, some fifty unusually keen students signed up. But the numbers rose disturbingly, first to about three hundred and then seven hundred. Without access to assistants who could mark the exercises, this kind of activity-oriented teaching functions badly. The conclusion, therefore, was that the alternative course had to be discontinued.

An assumption I particularly invoked in the years between 1939 and 1949 was that young students could make vital contributions to the teaching itself. If we treated philosophical questions that *they* felt to be relevant, their motivations would appreciably increase. Many of them proved willing to devote much of their time to the work of reform. But I also maintained that if they had wild, imaginative plans, they ought rather to realize *them* by traveling, for example. I must have overemphasized this point, because when the student committee reconvened after the summer vacation, barely half the members turned up. A familiar pattern in student life? Far from it. They had merely gone away. Some had gone to work in an Israeli kibbutz—a little society where everything was regulated with a strictness that was a profound contrast to Norwegian student life. A maturing experience, I should think.

In the ethics alternative most of the young students displayed a rich emotional engagement in relevant philosophical questions— and do so even more markedly today, as I gather from active teachers. And those students believe that it is important to have their own philosophical thoughts scrutinized. In addition, some of them experience a certain, albeit perhaps a modest, maturing of the emotional aspects of their standpoints, or at all events attain a certain insight into the direction such maturing process ought to take. "Where am I? What do I want?" are questions calculated to promote maturity, especially when students gather to work on their academic exercises in informal colloquia, or small, autonomous study groups, the leaders of which keep in touch with the teachers.

A clearer, well-articulated understanding of where one stands in relation to life's many dilemmas adds to the process of maturing. It is often of great help to become accustomed at an early age to writing down one's random thoughts, even if they lean toward whimsy. Unfortunately, many people have the feeling that it is pretentious to write, or that one has to reflect very carefully before doing so. But it is quite usual on the morrow to feel that what one wrote the day before is awkward and superficial. The main thing is that one managed to articulate one's thoughts at all, and in a way that invites improvement. Then later on, at leisure, one may achieve a *little* better expression of what one believes one espouses.

8 *The Art of Living: To Do Little Things in a Big Way*

Many older people have a great ability to take difficulties in their stride, while concentrating on what is important in life. Many young and middle-aged people are late in realizing this, because they do not take the time seriously to question their priorities. The great consideration is not exactly what one spends one's time on. The important thing is how one commits oneself, and what strength one devotes to it. In a sense, the art of living is to be able to do little things in a big way.

I feel justified not only in accepting life but in paying homage to it. However, as long as human beings cannot manage to abolish torture and even the more extreme kinds of poverty, there is a hollow ring when those, like me, who are not afflicted by such things talk about the silver lining, about life's many opportunities for happiness, or about how grateful "we" ought to be. For tens of thousands of people, their only wish is to die.

I do not believe that human nature blocks the means of abolishing torture and extreme poverty. If we examine the conditions for a rich life with simple means, we find no closed doors, but many doors are difficult to open. We must exert ourselves to push the obstacles out of the way. Antoine Nicolas de Condorcet (1743–94), a leading philosopher of the Enlightenment, has constantly been ridiculed for maintaining that there are no limits to the perfectibility of humankind. In my view we know of no definite limits.

We need a new Enlightenment with a faith in considerable changes where all sides of our industrial society are concerned, and consequently a belief in the solution of the problems of war, poverty, and the environmental crisis. But the two former have been with us for thousands of years, and we cannot expect the next century to bring total victory in those arenas. This applies also to our new goals, to preserve the richness and diversity of life on Earth. No one can say how badly things will turn out in the next century. Nonetheless, the future of humankind depends on which small contributions each single one of us can make here and now.

Something Good May Come Out of Something Bad

The expression "the art of living" has a long history and a plethora of usages; yet it plays a modest role when we talk about how we ought to live. Those who are accomplished in the art of living are symptomatically regarded as bons vivants—"good-lifers"—frivolous people who cheerfully help themselves to wine, sex, and song. To maintain that a bon vivant, whether a man or a woman, is ethically serious and responsible would cause astonishment.

I propose that the term "the art of living" be used in a way that makes it a worthy goal to be a bon vivant. We talk about the art of cooking, of conversation, of being a good loser, of being satisfied with what one has. In like manner, the art of living may be concerned with the art of coping with the many hurdles of life. The word *art,* and the related word *artist,* are unfortunate to the extent that they are associated with membership in an elite. I am using the word *art* in a sense that assumes that to practice the art of living is not elitist, not restricted to a narrow little circle.

I interpret being good at the art of living as having the ability to lead a life characterized by happiness—without reducing the chances of others to do the same. And a life may easily deserve to be called happy even if it is marked by a great many horrible events and sorrowful moments. There are many who can talk about the positive changes in life that occurred as the long-term effect of something unpleasant that happened. It is different with people who have an open wound for life after horrible events, and who are never the same after something terrible has happened.

Some people are especially lucky and privileged in their upbringing. This is connected with the surroundings, chances they had from infancy, talents that appeared early and were developed, and so on. Of others it is said that they had a miserable start, that they were unlucky in everything. Fate deals very differently with each of us.

In my sixties I finally became aware of the really great victories that many old people garner. The victories are great considering the cards that these people still hold. Many have rheumatoid arthritis, a bad back, or other painful afflictions, but surprisingly often they have kept their good humor and zest for life. They take care of themselves, of the pleasures they still have, and of their relations with other people. This is the art of living at its best. These people overcome disappointments that, in their twenties and thirties, would have angered them, perhaps even caused their mental collapse.

The feeling that things are getting better, that one is coping, even allowing for much less vitality, is one of the best feelings one can have. It is naturally unpleasant to admit to oneself that, strictly speaking, one is going downhill physically and mentally. That this is a natural part of life may be of some solace. But if a person is caught in a landslide and trapped with a foot under a rock, it is callous of someone who comes to his aid to say that, strictly speaking, accidents are only natural. For some people, that Nature is cruel is no consolation. It is merely generalizing what, in my view, is the dark side of life.

Therefore, my young readers (if any), think a little about all the things that many of your elders manage to overcome with good humor and give them recognition and support as often as you can. One of the best bon mots that I have discovered in the art of living is "It does not depend on how you are doing, but how you are coping."

Zapffe: The World Has No Meaning. It Is No Place for Human Beings

I think that it is worthwhile looking at the work of the aforementioned Peter Wessel Zapffe, a prominent Norwegian existential writer and philosopher. His views are important when dealing with the philosophy of the emotions and the art of living. He loved fishing and mountain climbing. He was a fabulous raconteur. But he classified all this as mere distraction. Why? He had an intense feeling that the living conditions he saw around him were not worthy of a sentient human being. And he considered that this was a *true* interpretation of the world. Such is the world: he thought that he had a metaphysical vision; an ability to penetrate a truth about the world that most people understandably refused to take seriously. When he was accused of arrogance, he answered that he did not consider himself infallible in any way, but that he was simply giving voice to his own personal conviction—which applied also to his assertion about vision. I will try to summarize Zapffe's position briefly.

Evolution has given humankind a brain with such a great capacity that we gradually understand that the world is utterly meaningless and unjust. We also grasp that absolutely everything is transient. That the possibility of something after death is nothing but wishful thinking. That if one insists on justice one is likely to end up in jail. People abhor the very thought of unwanted reality and therefore willingly allow themselves to be distracted by much that crosses their path. In the long run, nonetheless, they do not want to renounce a desire for justice and meaning in existence taken as a whole. As outer circumstances reinforce the awareness of this desire for meaning, human beings will decide to put so few children into the world that in the end they will quite simply become extinct.

Zapffe's position says little specifically about emotions. But his viewpoint was highly emotional and also evoked strong feelings in those who came to know it. It seemed provocative: "Where do *I* stand? I must consider seriously what he is saying." His viewpoint itself, however, took the form of an emotionally neutral observation of circumstances in reality: human nature *is* such that with a sufficient degree of reflection, people will inevitably say "No, thanks" to conditions proffered them. Theoretically it ought to be possible to adopt Zapffe's principles, listening evenhandedly to the demands of our nature. In practice one would need a strong emotional drive. I generally say that Zapffe was demanding but not really much of a pessimist. It emerges from his life and writings that concrete examples of injustice that he noticed, or that came to his attention in other ways, made a particularly deep impression on him.

As I interpret Zapffe, he would not have articulated his metaphysical vision unless at an early age he had already experienced revulsion at the attitude to life that he believed he saw around him in his own circles. He was expelled from high school for advocating ideas that, according to his teacher, belonged to the gutter: spiritually sullying ideas. Zapffe the atheist made sarcastic remarks about religious ideas. To those who suggested that his ideas were sick, he replied that it was not at all a psychiatrist's task to decide which ideas were sick and which healthy.

From a Spinozistic perspective one might say that Zapffe had a view of human nature based on the assumption that the conditions of life provided by Nature exclude humanity's ability to act and live in conformity with our own essence. Human beings make demands on Nature—for example, the demand for a possibility of achieving justice among people. It was difficult for me to say more to Zapffe, a good friend of mine, than that injustice did not make so deep an impression on me as on him. Injustice might well be significantly reduced and did not make me unreceptive to what I call life's intrinsic values. For his part, Zapffe rejected the idea that there is an intrinsic worth in love, listening to music, being together with friends, or enjoying a landscape. Life as a whole must never be neglected, whether one is in love or not.

Opponents of Zapffe's philosophy objected, among other things, that he was influenced too much by emotions and personal experience. His father was brutal, and he himself found no soul mates. Furthermore, he was criticized for depending too much on biology and too little on recognized philosophy—Plato, Kant, and so on. Whatever one's objections, Zapffe should be given credit for representing a significant philosophy of life. It is original and rigorously argued in his main work, which deals with the fundamental predicament of human life.

The Great in the Small

The art of living is to be able to work with small things in a big way. Is there a key to life that gives access to inner peace and happiness? This question seems to be central to the writings of the Swedish writer and Nobel Prize winner Pär Lagerkvist. His books *The Eternal Smile* and *A Guest of Reality* have meant much me. Somewhere Lagerkvist writes about his stay in southern Europe, in a village of the old kind. It lies on the top of a steep little hill. There, one day, he sees an old woman sitting and weaving a basket with a dignity that compels respect. She is engrossed in her work as if it were the only thing in life. Lagerkvist says, "Human beings are living here. A calm and happy people who understand how to carry out a life's work. To do small things in a big way."

I rarely have this impression in Scandinavia. Rather, we have the feeling that old men and women often do things of little significance, simply to have something to occupy them and while away the time. Whiling away time—what a horrible expression! Lagerkvist writes that "the people [in Scandinavia] do not have enough self-respect or respect for every deed."

Lagerkvist is a thinker, but as a novelist he can indeed express his thoughts without having to explain and justify them philosophically. As a philosopher, I alternate between social participation and detachment. I try to enter into the work of a writer, and try to use it as a starting point for thinking further. It can be easy enough to discover the philosophical value, but it is difficult to think *clearly* about the propositions suggested by an interpretation of Lagerkvist's sentences.

I am convinced that his literary works can greatly stimulate a young student of philosophy. As soon as the Philosophical Institute was established at the University of Oslo, I put my own copies of Ibsen's and Lagerkvist's books in the modest institute library. This did not lead to much debate, but I must take the blame for that. The students did not take care of the collection, so subsequently I took most of it back again. At any rate, the initiative was meant to help to humanize the abstractions of philosophy.

To someone infected by the philosophical bacillus, it is impossible to avoid seizing on the overwhelming questions related to existence and meaning. This can affect minor everyday concerns, which may then seem nonessential and distracting. But there are ways of avoiding the impression of a gulf between that which is of central importance and that which is simply the routine and drudgery needed to survive. I believe that many Norwegians do this by spending some of their time in their log cabins in the countryside. The classic Norwegian culture in these cabins involves so much simplicity and comprehensibility in the small everyday tasks that one feels respect for every deed one does. But only a very few are able to spend much time in a cabin, and some people seem to long for a more sophisticated existence after a few weeks with "simplicity of means."

As we have already seen, Spinoza classifies the state of being *hopeful* as a passive emotion. Such an unusual point of view may be defended on the grounds that a state of *merely* being hopeful does not activate the human essence. Insofar as it is enjoyable, it is a form of titillation. One should not wander about and merely hope that things will turn out well; one ought to do something about it. We do not put things in God's hands, for we *are* God's hands. Either we do something to realize our hopes, or we do what is useful *today*. The art of living appears to be concerned with seeing the greater whole in simple things and with being grateful for life in big and small things. But what is gratitude? Many people are pleased when others remember services they have performed. Now and then one may expect gratitude even if one has done nothing at all to deserve it. The feeling of gratitude has its own peculiarities in the same way as other feelings do. Some quotations from a little book called *Words of Gratitude,* published by the Danish writer Piet Hein in 1980, will illustrate this: "He who expects gratitude does not deserve it." And so will a Chinese proverb: "Forget the favors you have done; remember the gratitude you have received."

In the rich countries we need to shift our focus from standard of living to quality of life. The term *quality of life* is used here in the sense that it is used in research into the subject. It is an expression of how one looks upon one's life; how one feels and appreciates the world around one. In principle this is regarded as distinct from how much material goods one possesses. I am reminded of an old saying: "If you own more than three things, the things will own you." This is naturally an oversimplification, but by reducing our standard of living and the number of things with which we surround ourselves, we may actually raise the quality of life. By owning fewer things, we may also find it easier to achieve a better relationship with those few, essential things we have. If something goes wrong, we will repair the object instead of throwing it away and buying a new one. There may be much undiscovered quality of life in a rich life with simple means.

To illustrate this point, let us consider for a moment the life of a Polynesian of my acquaintance. His name is, approximately,

Avanaialaba. He is passionately keen on traveling and likes to visit different societies with varying customs. In a boat of his own construction, he sails far and wide with his family and a couple of close friends. At night he navigates in the classical way, by sitting absolutely still in the boat to sense the waves from different directions. In this way he avoids all the perilous coral reefs. His favorite food is raw flying fish, which he catches in full flight. He carries homemade musical instruments. In the communities that he visits, he supports himself as an odd-job man. He is good at navigation. He owns nothing except his own boat, but because he is such a helpful person, he is welcome everywhere. He has attained a high quality of life with simple means. But how does a modern society judge people like him?

King Olav, a Master of the Art of Living?

It would be interesting to ask a group of people to point out masters of the art of living among well-known historical figures and to ask why they consider that the people in question may justifiably be described as such. If the answer is no one, their justification would be interesting to hear.

Among royal families the late King Olav V of Norway is a natural choice for me, and for many other people. There is a delightful picture showing him staring at a cat with a broad smile on his face. Once, after I had given a short but not very successful after-dinner speech in the Norwegian coastal city of Bergen, I had the opportunity of asking King Olav about various things. When our conversation touched on the sense of loneliness, he frankly indicated that he had had some very difficult times. He maintained that it was very special being a king, especially after his life's companion had died. One is quite alone in many things and has few colleagues. One must follow royal protocol, everlastingly expressing interest and appreciation. King Olav managed to tread a fine line between displaying the common touch and satisfying the necessity of maintaining the dignity of a sovereign. And withal, he was a good ski jumper and a brilliant yachtsman.

At my request he expressed his willingness to become the patron of the Norwegian Mount Everest expedition in 1985. At the reception on the return of the expedition, small groups formed, each engaged in lively discussion. When King Olav approached to hear what was being said, people did not stand aside for the monarch. He found a suitable place himself. I had not expected this. He seemed to accept it in a *completely* relaxed manner.

Was he a master of the art of living? Or "just" an unusually accomplished person socially? Can anyone give most of the people a convincing impression of constant good humor without being something of a master of the art of living? I do not have the evidence to answer this question. What interests me is how many different kinds of human life it is possible to lead, even in a little country like Norway. The life of a king is only one of the extremes.

Until his last years Gandhi understood the art of living. Many people may possibly find this odd. He volunteered for a war waged by England against the Zulus in South Africa and became well known because he was forever cheerful. He was a stretcher bearer and seemed to like being in the danger zone, always smiling broadly. Later in life this special good mood of his became a huge asset when trying to resolve great conflicts. He could open a profoundly serious conference at the highest level with a joke, something that thawed the atmosphere on both sides of the conference table.

And he ate exactly what he felt like. He was not puritanical, but since his eating habits were always so peculiarly simple, they were often interpreted as asceticism or puritanism. He was, however, absolutely opposed to asceticism. His simplicity put its stamp on his whole way of life. He did not believe in the consumerist mentality, and his identifying himself with the poor deprived him surely of the taste for expensive pleasures. The poor can enjoy themselves, thoroughly and with much laughter, but without extravagance by our standards.

"Climbing is as meaningless as life itself," said Peter Wessel Zapffe, and kept on climbing. It gave him meaning to tell people that life is meaningless. Fishing and climbing might well produce pleasant feeling but nonetheless lacked meaning. That something felt good was not an adequate proof of meaning to him. Many people have the same attitude. Some people experience certain phases— for example, the last phase of life before death—as situations from which both the positive emotions and all meaning are absent. To me it seems academic in a pejorative sense to say which is worst as a matter of principle. My aim was to reflect on the relation between feeling and meaning. That life is meaningful is a necessary but not sufficient condition for a life consistent with human dignity.

Seen from the outside, a meaningful life can turn out to be marked by sorrow and pain. A good, satisfying job may be dependent on outside circumstances that make a proper execution of the job possible. If the outer circumstances continually become more difficult, it may mean that a post that previously seemed a bottomless source of pleasure has ceased to be so. One is disheartened by all the setbacks. The conditions for deriving satisfaction from the job have gradually disappeared. There is nothing to guarantee a stable, high quality of life any longer. The characteristic of work that feels positive is joy. When joy is involved, you want to do more of the same work.

As human beings, we have no *guarantee* that the future will resemble the past. Our formulations of natural "laws" are based on observations of the past. We cannot, therefore, guarantee how we will feel in the future. However, given the unimaginable number of possibilities, the absence of such a guarantee is of no practical consequence. Contemplating the lack of guarantee may, however, color our view of life—of the strange human predicament.

There is no limit to the durability of an emotion when it originates deep inside one. As an example, consider Mother Teresa. By her own account, her strength came from a living religious faith. Doctors who survived the Hiroshima atom bomb tried to carry out their medical duties without hospitals, without medicines. It was an attempt to do something with a sense of purpose under almost completely impossible circumstances.

Joy

It is now twenty-eight years since I gave my farewell address as a professor. It was in the ceremonial hall of the University in Oslo. Before I spoke, diplomas were presented to older, unhappy-looking students who had finally graduated. Some of them already looked washed out. The title of my address was, quite simply, "Joy." The address aroused an interest I have rarely seen. I will try to present some of my thoughts on the subject. In my view of the world, joy has a place as important as love and happiness, perhaps even more so.

What I want to say is yet again inspired by Spinoza. If I concentrate on the subject of joy, it is because it is not fully accepted in many crucial situations where it ought to be respected. Sometimes it is decried as superficial—it is said to displace deliberate consideration of cruel circumstances and forces that beset humanity. To me, Spinoza's "philosophy of joy" is a great inspiration. Spinoza seems to conceive of a state of joy basically as a process, not a sensation. To be full of joy is to take pleasure in the world as it appears to you at the moment. You experience a joyful "world," and therefore something that (ontologically speaking) *is* joyful, not something only inside you. The world and you cannot be completely separated from each other.

According to Spinoza there are two main kinds of joy: *titillatio* and *hilaritas.* Put simply, *hilaritas* fills the whole person, all parts of the body and soul. In the case of *titillatio,* only parts of the self are affected. In other words, *titillatio* is the joy that engages only parts of the body and parts of the soul, while *hilaritas* engages the whole person.

There can be too much *titillatio,* because it can easily block the capacity for other kinds of joy. According to Spinoza, *hilaritas* is the only joy of which there can never be too much. On the other hand, there can be too much of *amor,* which he defines in such a way that it is mere *titillatio;* it may not come from the whole person. One who is engrossed in a superficial infatuation, for instance, may be engaged in pleasurable activities around the clock, but does infatuation embrace all aspects of that person's life? No. Does such an infatuation block certain aspects of the development of life? Yes. On the other hand, love of the creative force in existence and love of God—*amor intellectualis Dei*—is a type of *hilaritas.* There can quite simply not be too much of it.

I cannot come closer to an image of someone in constant *hilaritas* than by pointing to statues of Buddha, where the sculptor has only hinted at a smile. Otherwise the figure shows utter peace, devoid of passive emotions. This latter is important, because Spinoza talks about an inner peace that is consistent with an intense need for outer activity and display of joy. Speaking of this subject reminds me of something I have read about Sir Richard Burton's (1821–90) expedition to find the source of the "white" Nile. He was met with all sorts of mishaps and suffered physical pain and diseases. But he kept enough of his calm to go on with the search. He developed the essence of his nature and was in a positive mental state all the time. Burton belongs to those who fascinate us but who seem immature and are not highly developed emotionally. He was daring: as a diplomat he quite suddenly published (very good) translations of pornography or, more correctly, works of oriental sexual art and wisdom, thereby risking imprisonment! Mature or not, his life makes joyful reading. But do we love his recklessness or immaturity?

Spinoza maintains that it is joy that allows his eight goals and values (see Chapter 4) to be followed to different degrees. Joy is also internally related to freedom, power, and understanding—it cannot be defined conclusively without referring to other phenomena. In other words, joy is a phenomenon that must be considered within a network of different relationships. Spinoza seeks a kind of joy that is not, as it were, pasted to the real target, but rather forms a whole together with it. Consequently, he can speak of something as peculiar as human beings' perfection increasing through joy. "If you are in a state of joy, you increase in perfection, and if you increase in perfection, you are in a state of joy." This depends on what is meant by perfection *(perfectio)*. Spinoza uses it in its fundamental sense of "realizing a goal."

Joy Is a Process That Changes One

Spinoza talks about joy as a process through whose agency one is changed. He says nothing about the sensation of joy itself. There is nothing to suggest that he undervalues this sensation or denies its existence, but above all it is a kind of process about which he wants to talk. *Joyful* is an adjective that describes how the world is felt, not a description of a feeling. To those with a bright temperament, what happens in the world appears bright. What occurs is no feeling but a change in the perception of the world.

Spinoza often considers questions relating to *potentia,* "power." Based on his philosophy of joy and the active emotions, which color the unfolding of human nature and essence, he maintains that he who acts with joy is "mightier," and more capable of attaining his goals, than he who, under like circumstances, acts out of hatred, distaste, or other passive emotions. Many people today complain of rising pressure from their surroundings. In Spinoza's terminology being under pressure means a sense of being powerless in certain relations and situations. And of course it also means lack of freedom. Spinoza's *homo liber*—literally "free man"—is a human being whose decisions are effectively under his own control and not determined by outside pressures.

In discussing the relation between joy and power, Spinoza naturally considers "the power to," not "power over." "The power to" is the power to attain one's goals when one acts in accordance with one's innermost nature. "Power over" is the power to compel others to make decisions and act in the way decided by the person exercising that power.

Spinoza also has other fundamental things to say about joy, particularly about its more specialized forms. Satisfaction at work cannot be included; it may develop into a kind of disease if it dominates completely. In connection with satisfaction and advancement at work, I think particularly of those cases that have become ever more common in recent years: so-called happy and successful people who go to psychiatrists and complain about lacking the joy of life. We have now become painfully aware that success and a high standard of living do not necessarily lead to a high quality of life.

If Spinoza is right, we must try to maintain lasting joy as the prevailing tone in our emotional life. To borrow again an analogy from skiing, it is somewhat like the base wax with which we prepare the soles of our skis. On top of this adhesive base, we add various waxes according to the snow conditions. There are many factors that can make people feel that their lives are somewhat too chaotic, that they are a prey to their emotions, driven rudderless around, and naturally the dominant tone is not very stable, and often negative. It may also be oppressive to be steered too much by habit, to be too strictly supervised. But people in the rich industrialized countries seem to complain more frequently about chaos. A word that is often used is *integrate,* that is to say, to turn something into a whole or a unit. We do not want to be uncertain or confused, or not to know where we are going; we wish to be integrated people.

The feeling of joy does not merely entail a transition to greater perfection, but is also concerned with a necessary, internal relation to the transition itself. How? In Spinoza's day, and in his surroundings, there was not our sharp distinction between a feeling and the object of that feeling. People were then unfamiliar with the belief that there are feelings of joy that can be isolated from the object of which one is fond or for which one has a strong feeling. They did not think, "Here we have a flower with certain characteristics like diameter and height—and then we have the joy of looking at it." No, the flower itself *is* joyful. We ourselves, the flower as we spontaneously appreciate it, and the pleasure itself together form an indestructible whole. Technically it may be called a gestalt; an entity that cannot be arbitrarily separated into subject, object, and medium. This means not only that joy entails a transition to greater perfection, but that it is *included* in that state of perfection in a more intimate way.

Am I Happy with the Particular Kind of Life I Lead?

Sometimes we are unhappy and we feel it is quite unjustified. The reason often seems to be that we do not manage to keep a long-term goal sufficiently clear and continuously in our sights. Perhaps the means of attaining the goal have become painful. Or they seem repulsively boring because we do not keep repeating to ourselves what our long-term goal is. Or we choose goals that are too distant, given our level of integration, how concentrated we are, how willing we are to maintain a particular way of life. Some people are noticeably stable from their earliest years, almost monomaniac. Others need change, always something new, but nonetheless cope brilliantly. Others again fall ill when their powers are not great enough to continue their usual way of life.

We must really ask ourselves this question to a greater extent: Am I happy with this kind of life now, and is what I am doing necessary for that which I conceive to be the good life? If we consistently answer in the negative, we ought if necessary to take radical steps to change direction and do something else. Or we ought to try to understand what we are doing in a different way. In that case we have to put life and activities in a different context.

Why did I retire from my university chair in 1969, twelve years before it was necessary? It was not because the company of students and colleagues no longer gave me any pleasure, but because I believed, and still believe, that one is ground down as a person by keeping a job that demands much time and attention, and where routine plays too great a role. I felt that I was functioning more than living. Most activities had to conform to a timetable. On one occasion I wondered why I did not walk down to the harbor and simply board a banana boat and finish up in some exotic place or other as a lay preacher. I could not stop indulging in fantasies of extensive breaks in my deadening routine.

When I announced that I wanted to retire, there was speculation in many quarters about the reason. Some people thought that the "student revolution" had been too trying. Although I naturally disagreed with much of what the radical student leaders believed in, I found the events invigorating. Believing that some people might discover the real reasons for my retiring, I put out a statement through the Norwegian news agency that I "wanted to live rather than function." Today it is encouraging to see that many people jump off the train in which they have been traveling too long.

But leaving the university did not lead to any personal upheaval for me. I became extremely active in the environmental movement. But also there, dissidence was inhibited: new stimuli were controlled too strictly without one's realizing it. I mention this because a commitment that starts in a blaze of light can falter, and we ourselves lose the spark and the ability to inspire others. It is of some help to be aware that this is something that is happening and consciously try to find new paths to renewal.

Yet again I have written about my own decisions. My justification is that I ought to be able to get a fairly clear idea of the function of feelings in the processes leading to decision. What was the role played by plain facts and assumed self-knowledge? It is my contention that the role of these intellectual factors is generally overrated, and that on the whole we may perhaps be glad that we are not aware of the many emotional roots of our decisions. If we were more aware of this, the high status of knowledge would make us invent facts to support our decisions. I would call my decision to quit my job fairly rational, that is to say, neither rational nor irrational. The vague expression "to want to live rather than function" suggests a rational choice. And of course it is a socially acceptable simplification of an immensely complex structure of reasoning and feeling.

The Role of Play in Life

It is obvious that in the eyes of the world, a practitioner of the art of living is rarely if ever expected to take life seriously. There must be room for self-irony, humor, and play. People who take the time to read what I am writing presumably fail all too often to follow playful impulses that could bring them pleasure. I believe that learning to relax would be a pleasant surprise for many people who take the ethical dimension too seriously.

On the other hand, it is encouraging to imagine oneself as a possible bon vivant who also "takes the serious seriously"—an expression that Harald Ofstad, a Norwegian moral philosopher, often used. The real point is whether we can allow ourselves to seek the art of living boldly. Or does it mean that we are already on a perilous path? My answer is that it does not. Nor does it necessarily mean that, to take an example, we ought to go to more parties, or anything as definite as that. The art of living is displayed both at work and in everyday life.

But what about play? For most of us life is far from being a kind of game. The need to be responsible and strive to attain set goals makes it difficult for many to find the metaphor appropriate. Nonetheless, people like me are sometimes described as believing that everything is more or less a game. This seems to me a little odd, but, on the bright side, it has led to my often being urged to reflect on how much of life can and ought to have the character of play in spite of life's earnestness. Incidentally, it is essential to draw a distinction between a game and play. A game may have strict rules, with competition sometimes at the core. Playfulness has more to do with expressions of good humor and personal creativity.

The expression "the playful human being," *homo ludens* in Latin, arouses varying feelings. For my part, I am prone to associate it with superficiality and irresponsibility. A human being might perhaps be called *homo ludens* even if he considers human life to be extremely serious—as long as he is constantly in search of, and finds opportunities for, play. The Austrian philosopher Moritz Schlick (1882–1936), one of the prominent figures in the Vienna circle, declared himself to be an adherent of the view that life is a game. Some of us who knew him were tempted to interpret this as revealing a deep longing. He himself seemed never to find time to play and rarely smiled with us.

In an article on the meaning of life, Schlick maintained that human beings have a tendency to work toward goals that no longer mean anything to us when we finally attain them. On the contrary, attaining that kind of a goal usually results in inconsolability and loneliness. We will never, for example, find "the meaning of life" in work. Nor will we find it if we look for beauty and truth. But *play,* defined as any activity that takes place for its own sake, "reveals" the meaning of life. Except in childhood, human beings live "under the curse of goals." Playfulness can very well be involved in many more situations in everyday life. If one is setting a table, there are dozens of more or less grand gestures with which one can accompany the task. Staircases are and always will be delightful challenges. But even so commonplace a thing (for a professor) as giving a lecture is a serious matter, and considerations of many kinds characterize the preparations and delivery. It is alleged that I often seemed unprepared in the approximately four thousand lectures that I delivered as a professor at the University of Oslo. That may well be true, and I am not exactly proud of it. Very likely the lectures seemed child's play to me, but so much the worse for the outcome.

A Formula for Well-Being

Keep the fervor of life. It is tempting to say this now that we are after all in a kind of final-word mood. Luckily we can be deeply committed to something, to a subject, a pastime, a competitive activity, without the necessity of "becoming someone" or carrying that which we are doing through to some predetermined goal. When we notice that there is something that sets us aflame, it is advisable to form a fairly realistic estimate of the *durability* of this interest. Here I should like to propose a formula that expresses what it means to maintain that flame, glow, or fervor, whether it applies to something professional or something quite personal:

$$T = \frac{G^2}{L_l + L_s}$$

T stands for the level of well-being

G stands for the flame, glow or fervor

L_l stands for physical suffering

L_s stands for mental suffering

If the intensity varies from 1 to 100, maximum fervor guarantees a high degree of well-being despite a great deal of mental and physical suffering. Supposing we substitute the figure 100 for fervor, and the same value for mental and physical suffering. If you have the same amount of fervor as suffering, the fervor is nonetheless always the most decisive for well-being: In this case the numerator is 10,000, only 200 for the denominator, and a well-being value of 50. If physical and mental suffering rise dramatically, let us say by 100 each, and the fervor rises by only 50, well-being rises nonetheless. On the other hand, if the fervor is miserable, well-being must be miserable irrespective of how small the discomforts that arise.

If the fervor is great, we can withstand great strains of both a mental and physical kind. Therefore it is so important to concentrate particularly on the glow or fervor. It counts not only in sports and on expeditions, but in friendship, marriage, and all creative activity. If we observe that something or other causes a more intense engagement, we must take care of these circumstances. If as a result of the formula the fervor rises from 3 to 4 or 6, a great deal of pain is required to threaten well-being.

History is full of tales of heroism. Heroism demands fervor. Martyrs of all religions have met death with a smile. When Winston Churchill, very ill, very late in life, managed to put on his slippers by himself, he gave the V sign. He was celebrating a victory—in my view, a very real victory. It is not a question of how much we manage—of whether we are engaged in something big or small—but of whether there is still something at which we can smile: some victories.